Sermons on Those Other Special Days

SERMONS
ON THOSE
OTHER
SPECIAL
DAYS

HUGH LITCHFIELD

BROADMAN PRESS
Nashville, Tennessee

ISBN: 0-8054-2120-3
Dewey Decimal Classification: 252.6
Subject Heading: CHURCH YEAR - SERMONS
Library of Congress Catalog Number: 89-34996

Printed in the United States of America

Unless otherwise stated, all Scripture quotations are from the *Revised Standard Version of the Bible,* copyrighted 1946, 1952, © 1971, 1973.

Scripture quotations marked NASB are from the *New American Standard Bible.* © The Lockman Foundation, 1960, 1962, 1963, 1968, 1971, 1972, 1973, 1975, 1977. Used by permission.

Library of Congress Cataloging-in-Publication Data

Litchfield, Hugh, 1940-
    Sermons on those other special days / Hugh Litchfield.
       p. cm.
    ISBN 0-8054-2120-3 :
    1. Occasional sermons. 2. Sermons, American. 3. Baptists-
-Sermons. I. Title.
BV4254.2.L57   1990
252'.67—dc20

                          89-34996
                            CIP

To the people who were and are
Azalea Baptist Church,
Norfolk, Virginia,
"Thanks for the memories"
(1971-1988)

Contents

Preface

Introduction: Those Other Special Days

Preface

Preaching is an exciting adventure. To be privileged to speak in behalf of the Lord is both a blessing and an awesome responsibility. Will we preach the right word? Will we say it well? Will we be heard, or will we be ignored as having no word worthy for our time?

As a pastor of one church for seventeen years, and now as a teacher of preaching and preachers, these questions weave their way through my mind. How can we touch the real lives of our people?

One way I feel we can is to preach on many of the special days of the year. The Christian faith concerns all of life, and to bring a Christian perspective to the special emphases of life can be a timely word for now. This is what this book is about. Previously, I have shared ways to preach the Christmas and Easter stories. This book will hopefully help to point to ways that we can preach on some of the "other" special days, to deal with some of the other stories that make up our lives.

I appreciate both the congregation of the Azalea Baptist Church of Norfolk, Virginia, and my colleagues and students of the North American Baptist Seminary of Sioux Falls, South Dakota, for their encouragement and support as I have sought to teach and preach. They mean more to me than words can ever express.

I wish also to thank Muriel Hoggard for her tireless work in typing the manuscript. She has been a good and patient coworker. I am in debt to her for her excellent work.

Introduction:
Those Other Special Days

Each day of the year is significant. It is a day given to us by God, a gift from His hand. There are some days that hold extra significance because of some memorable idea or event connected with them. We call them "special days," days filled with special meaning and celebrations.

At times, there seem to be too many special days. Almost every Sunday seems to have some special emphasis connected with it. As pastors, there may be those moments when we throw up our hands and want to forget them all. What do we do with the special days that come down the road? Do we ignore them? Do we preach on *all* of them?

Somewhere between those two extremes, most of us plant our feet. We somehow feel that there are *some* special days we should preach on. However, we must pick and choose. Which ones should get that special treatment, which ones should be forgotten?

This is my experience through seventeen years as pastor of one church. There were the days that seemed to lend themselves to special treatment, the ones that the people seemed to be concerned about. Others may choose to add other days, or to omit some of mine. It is my hope that this book will stir your imagination as to what might be done about the other special days that keep coming year after year.

I have said "other" because most of us already preach on the truly special days of our faith. We cannot omit preaching on

Christmas, Thanksgiving, or Easter. But what about those days in between? What will we do with them?

I have chosen to divide my choices under two main headings.

General Days

There are general special days, days with no special religious significance attached. These days are celebrated outside the religious community. Almost everyone gives some attention to them and at least thinks about them briefly. But they may not think about these days from a religious or faith perspective.

Our challenge is to help people celebrate these special days within some religious framework. We must seek to show how such a day can be a means to understanding, celebrating, and doing the grace of God. Building on the already familiar foundations of the special day, we can structure a perspective of faith that can give the day some special meaning.

From the many days, I have chosen seven.

(1) New Year's Day

"If only I could start all over again." How many times has that cry been heard from human lips? We all would like a place of beginning again, where we could get another chance to do and be what we should. New Year's Day reminds us that we do get such a chance. The beginning of a New Year focuses our attention on the possibilities of starting over, of doing it better this time.

The gospel is a gospel of second chances, of starting over again. How easily this can be applied to New Year's Day. Sermons could capitalize on the chance that God gives us to really start over, the mercy that helps us to change for the better. The truth is there— we can be better than we were!

(2) Valentine's Day

This day zeroes in on the idea of expressing our love to one another. But what is love? It has been used to describe everything from the basest pornography to the death of Christ on the cross. What an opportunity Valentine's Day provides to explore the nature and character of Christian love! There is no love like His love, and we can help others understand that.

(3) Baccalaureate Day

In some communities, it is no longer traditional to have a Baccalaureate Sunday for graduating students. However, almost every church sets aside a Sunday to recognize graduates among their membership. Why not a sermon on the meaning of graduation and education? Such a sermon can help provide graduates with some vision and insight on what they are going to face in the years to come.

(4) Children's Day

Recently the celebration of a children's day has gained great recognition. In the church, we need to celebrate the gifts from God that our children are. We need to remember the hope they signify. There is much to learn about children and from children. They can truly be our teachers.

(5) Memorial Day

This day helps us remember the sacrifice that others have made on our behalf. We are debtors to so many. This day can also be a time when we recall the greatest sacrifice made for us: the sacrifice of Christ on the cross. We are indeed debtors to Him.

(6) July Fourth

This is a special day in the life of our nation. This day will certainly be celebrated, for we are proud of our heritage as Americans. What does this day have to say to us as Christians, citizens of the kingdom of God? This day can be used to discuss the meaning of Christian citizenship and patriotism. It can also be a vehicle to the understanding of freedom. What does it mean to be truly free? As we celebrate the birthday of America, we need to seek to give some religious perspectives to it.

(7) Labor Day

While most work, many do not enjoy it. Work has become something to endure, not to enjoy. We need a new perspective about our work. Is there a Christian one? Labor Day is a good chance to recapture the meaning of work—under God.

Special Church Days

Within the life of the church, special emphases and programs are presented. Often the pastor is expected to preach on these issues. Such days do provide important opportunities to bring the light of the gospel to bear on these promotions.

(1) Parent/Child Dedication

Within churchs which do not practice infant baptism, parent/child dedication services have become quite prominent. In these services, parents dedicate their child to God while, at the same time, dedicating themselves to being parents who will seek to train their children in the ways of God. The whole church should affirm the desire of the parents and pledge to do what it can to see the dreams of the parents come true.

(2) Pentecost Sunday

This Sunday is often neglected in many churches. Tradition dates Pentecost as the beginning of the Christian church. The day commemorates a significant event in the history of our faith that provides an opportunity to educate people on the nature and purpose of the New Testament church. A teaching sermon on the meaning of Pentecost would be helpful.

(3) Ascension Sunday

As it was with Pentecost, often the Ascension experience is neglected in the worship of the church. For many, this event does seem to be "out of this world," unrelated to life today. Sermons are needed that capture the hope and triumph of Christ that the moment signifies. Preaching on the Ascension is a much-needed word for our time.

(4) Stewardship Sunday

As much as we may wish otherwise, the church does need the voluntary gifts of its members: their time, talents, and financial contributions. Budgets have to be raised, and the pastor plays an important part in that. We must "preach on money." How can we do that tactfully, honestly, without turning people off? That is a tough challenge, but we must keep the gospel message on stewardship alive.

(5) Mission Sunday

We are to spread the gospel everywhere. We all know that. We need to call for missionaries to go and for the financial support needed for them when they do. Mission work at home and abroad is the work of the church. If a church loses its vision for missions, it will suffer. The privilege is ours to preach on missions.

(6) Communion Sunday

The service of the Lord's Supper must not be an addendum to a worship service. It is the gospel for the eye and the message it presents is the heart of the gospel. In many churches Communion is usually celebrated once a month or once a quarter. When it is celebrated, the sermon should be related to the meaning of the Supper. The Word and the Elements can work together to powerfully present the gospel. We need to strive in our sermons to probe the unending depths of its meaning. It is a word for life.

Conclusion

This book contains some representative sermons on those "other" special days. I make no claim that this is the only way to do it or the best way to do it. This is just one pastor's attempt to make the special days significant for the faith. But if I can stimulate you to think about how you might preach on these days, I feel my hope for this book will not have been in vain.

If these sermons are helpful, to God be the glory! For when all is said and done, His grace has made every day special. In response to what He has done, is doing, and will do, we have a special message for any day, anytime. Thanks be to God!

Part I:
General Days

1
New Year's Day:
The Choice We Will Face

(Josh. 24:14-18)

Most people laugh when we talk about New Year's resolutions. They don't take them seriously anymore. The attitude seems to be: "What's the use to make them, we're only going to break them!" So we don't talk much about making New Year's resolutions. That could be a mistake because I feel there is value in making them. For one thing, it reminds us that there are areas of our lives that need to be improved. We are not all that we need to be; we are not perfect. We need to do something about improving our lives. In order to change, we've got to face those areas where we need to change. The making of resolutions can sometimes help us do that.

I think, too, that the making of resolutions reminds us that we are responsible for what we make of our lives. If there are areas of our lives that need to be changed, we can make decisions about whether or not we want to change them. We can quit going through life blaming others about what we have become and start assuming responsibility for what we make out of our lives. We have the freedom to choose what we become. Growing toward maturity is learning to accept responsibility for our lives.

I don't know what resolutions you might have made or need to make, but at one time in our lives, most of us have made this resolution. We resolved that we would be a Christian. We resolved that we would try to the best of our ability to serve Christ and do what He wanted. In the year ahead, that resolution will be tested and tried. It is easier to make a resolution than to keep one. We will come across many experiences in the year ahead that will ask us whether we mean that resolution. We will have to choose. Will we serve God or not? It is similar to the experience that Joshua had in this farewell speech when he told the people they had to make a decision. They would have to choose to serve God or not. They had to make up their minds on that. So do we. In the days ahead, there will be several times when we will have to decide: Will we choose to serve Christ or not to serve Him?

I. Will we choose to serve Christ when temptations come?

In Joshua's day, there were many voices calling for the allegiance of the people—many false gods. Joshua mentioned the gods that lived in Egypt or the gods of the Ammorites (v. 14-18). They were false gods calling for people to indulge in pleasure and the pursuit of their own passions. They would have to choose whether or not they would trust those gods or whether they would trust the God they had known, the God who had brought them out of Egypt and brought them into the Promised Land. The problem with the false gods was that they looked enticing and promised so much. Joshua would say that in the end, they would deliver only boredom and emptiness. But they had to decide which God they would serve? Which God or god would they trust for life?

They would have to choose, and so do we. In our day there are many false gods calling for our attention. The problem with them is that they do look enticing, and their words are like honey, sweet to our hearing. They can easily persuade us that they know the key to life and the joy and happiness of it. These gods are many. *Materialism* tells us that the way to life is found in things. The more we have the merrier we will be. We often buy that, and we go after the pursuit of things: televisions, clothes, cars, and houses. The more we amass, the happier we feel we will be. It sounds so right, and many of us spend our lives in the pursuit of things.

There is the god of *pleasure* who tries to convince us that life is just meant to be one big party. You've got to do what you feel, do what comes naturally, do what you want. Go ahead! It's all right to take drugs and alcohol and stay high. If it feels good, do it! You don't have to worry about the idea that sex is supposed to be confined to a relationship of marriage where two people have committed themselves to one another for life. It's not for that. Forget it. In fact, forget about long-term relationships at all. After all, people are there for our pleasure. They are to bring us joy and happiness. If they don't, forget them. Anything that brings us a blast, do it. That sounds so tempting. We all want to have a good time. We all want to feel good. It's easy to follow that god.

The god *success* tells us that making it to the top is all that matters. You need to take it no matter what the price: family, friends, even your own personal integrity. Nobody cares about losing; nobody cares about who is number two. All that matters is who is number one. So don't let anybody or anyone stand in your way of making it to the top. When you get there, you will have power and people will be at your beck and call. It's really great to be at the top, to have that power. That's where life is found and it sounds so enticing.

The *popularity* god tells us that being with the "in" crowd is where it's at. Just find the majority opinion and go with it. Nobody wants to be left out anyway. We all want to be part of something, so we compromise and do what others want us to do because that's the way to life. We'll have a whole lot of friends draped around us. (By the way, that's only as long as we do what they want.) Maybe we can get elected president of the Student Council or Homecoming Queen or the captain of the football squad, for this is where life is found, being "in," being popular, and being one of the gang.

The gods call out to us. They sound so sweet, we can easily fall for their seduction. Then the voice of *God* comes to us and, in light of all of those other voices, the voice of God sounds so tame. God tells us that *things* won't bring us life. We must never come *under* the control of things, we must be *in* control of things. We can have all the stuff in life that we can gather, but they will only bring us emptiness. God tells us that to give way to our passions will lead to our destruction because we become a slave of our emotions instead of being in control. The pursuit of pleasure for pleasure's sake will one day leave us empty. God tells us that to be a success is not the goal of life: to be a servant is. It's lonely at the top. When we make it to the top, it's not all it was supposed to be. Life is found not worrying about being number one, but worrying about being a servant. Being popular? God tells us that's not important. What is important is being right, being decent, being morally strong. When we get down to it, being popular can leave us empty and confused inside.

But we will have to decide. Sometime this year, those temptations will come. Will we keep our resolution to be His children?

In French history there was a young boy who would have been King Louis XVIII. They gave him to a lady named Meg for training. She was supposed to train him to be evil, to lie, and to steal. They wanted to corrupt the boy because they didn't want him to become king. So he went to live with Meg, and he lived in rags and ate garbage trying to survive, but whenever she tried to teach him to lie and to steal, the boy would stamp his feet and rebel against it. He said, "I will not! I will not! I was born to be a king. A king will not do those things!"[1]

We have been born to be children of God. Are there some temptations we will not give into? It will be our decision when the temptations come. Will we serve God or not?

II. Will we choose to serve God when the testing comes?

The children of Israel had to face that problem then. To live in the Promised Land would not be easy. When it was hard to serve God, would they still hold on to Him? Their forefathers had some trouble with that. They had gotten to the edge of the Promised Land, scouted it out, and discovered that there were giants in the land, and they didn't like that at all. They wanted the Promised Land, but they wanted God to give it to them on a silver platter. They didn't want to have to work for it and to fight for it. When they discovered they might have to fight, they began to complain against God and accuse Him of misleading them. They never went into the Promised Land. These, their children, would have to decide. Would they stay with God when the battles came? Would they stay with God when it was hard to stay with God? Would they still choose Him?

Many in the year ahead will have to face that choice. The times of testing may not come to all of us, but I guarantee they will come to many of us. They come in different ways. It may be the loss of a loved one, for it's hard to let go and go on. It may be some sickness that won't go away and the pain frustrates and angers us. It may be a terrible disappointment that beats us down, the loss of a secure job, a girlfriend, boyfriend, or a marriage. Maybe it's a failure you can't seem to get over. Maybe a child runs away. Maybe a financial setback causes us to struggle just to make ends meet. These unwelcome visitors to our lives come in all sizes and shapes, but come they will and when they do, we have to decide. Will we trust God in the midst of them or not?

It is sad to say, many don't. When the tough times come, many give up on God. They cry out, "Why did God do this to me? If this is the way God works, I want to have no part of Him." Such a statement shows a tremendous misunderstanding of God and what He has promised us. For God has not promised us that He would magically make all of our problems disappear. He *has* promised to be with us in the midst of them, to help us face them, and to walk through them. Will we trust God to do that? When it gets tough, will we run from Him and follow Him no more? It will be our choice when the difficult testing times come. Will we still resolve to hold on to Him, even when it's hard?

There was a shepherd boy named Hans, a good shepherd boy. He took care of his flock well. But late one afternoon, he was behind a mountain and a blinding windstorm arose. Hans knew that he had to get the flock back home, but to do it, he knew they had to go right into the face of the wind. If they ran away from the storm and the wind, the wind would blow the wool of the sheep up, and the snow would get in, form ice, and eventually freeze them to death. His father had taught Hans that whenever a storm was coming, keep on going into the face of it, so that's what he tried to do. He tried to drive the sheep forward. He got his dog to nip the heels of them and keep them going into the face of the storm, as hard as it was. It was hard for him, too. It blew hard against him and he could hardly see. It caused him pain, but he kept on in the face of the wind and of the storm. Finally, his father and brothers who had come out to find him were able to help get the flock to safety. Later, over a hot supper, the father said, "We were worried about you out there." The young boy said, "Father, I did what you always told me to do. I kept going on in the face of the storm."[2]

God has told us that in the face of the storm, He will help us face it. When it hits us this year, will we trust Him and keep on going on with Him?

III. Will we trust Him and choose Him when the triumphs come?

You may say that sounds strange, but not really. One of the great problems of Joshua's people was their triumphs. Some of the greatest temptations come on the heels of some of their greatest victories. Some of the victories they gained quite easily, and they began to forget who gave them the victory. They began to trust in their own cleverness and their own abilities and less in God. Pride in themselves overtook humility and dependence upon the grace of God. Eventually, this was to be their downfall. They began to feel they didn't really need God, things were going pretty good. They were able to handle things on their own. So they quit depending on God until they woke up one day to discover that

God had become a stranger to them. They were weak and could not go on.

For us, the same temptations will be there. When the storms come, it is easy to realize our need of God, but when the sun is shining, it's easy to forget our need of Him. When everything is going well, we can forget who is the Source of it going well. Why do we need God when things are good?

Here is a dramatic illustration about a man in Texas I knew. He was young, with a lovely wife and daughter, a good job, a good bank account, a member of all the right clubs, but he made the statement, "I don't need God. I don't need church. Why do I need it? I have what I need." One night on a rainy road in a car accident, his wife and daughter were killed. He still had his job and his bank accounts, and he still had the membership in the country club, but he reached inside to find something to help him face what had happened and he found nothing, only emptiness.

Are things going well for you? Thank God for that, but never get to the place where you feel that they are going well because of your cleverness, because of your goodness, or because you deserve it. Remember that the sun shines today, but the storms of life can come up so quickly. What you ought to remember is every day of our life is a gift from the hand of God, and every day when things go well it is because of the grace of God. You must remember that who you are and what you will ever be is because of who He has been to you, what He is to you, and what He will be to you. May you never get to the place when things are going so well that you ignore Him. When things are going well, especially then, may you choose to rededicate yourself in thanksgiving to the God who has blessed you.

William Beebe was a friend of Theodore Roosevelt, and every now and then when things were going a bit tough with the president, they would go camping and would go through this ritual all of the time. At nighttime, Beebe would look up and say, "Near the stars where Pegasus is, there's a great spiral. It is as large as the

Milky Way. It is one of a 100 million galaxies, it is 750,000 light-years away, it has a 100 billion suns, each one of those suns bigger than our sun." After reciting those figures, Theodore Roosevelt would say, "Well, I think now we are small enough. Let us go on to bed."[3] Sometimes we forget who we are. We're not the Creator; we are the *created*. We walk by grace and by gift, and may every day this year we remember that and if things are going good each day, thank God that they are.

So the year lies ahead for us. Most of us have resolved to try to be Christian and that resolve will be tested. We will have to live it, and Joshua said we must choose who we will serve. Joshua said, "[I don't know who you're going to choose], but as for me and my house, we will serve the Lord" (v. 15). And he did. Most of us have said, "That's us. We've chosen to serve Him." Will we continue to choose to serve Him when the temptations come, and the testings come, even when the triumphs come? In all of those experiences, will we still hold on to Him?

Cliff Harris, a well-known preacher, spoke in a prison. A prisoner introduced him. He said, "Several years ago in the same neighborhood two boys grew up. They went to the same schools, played on the same ball team; they went to the same Sunday School and church. But one of those boys got smart and said he didn't need church and Sunday School anymore, and he quit going. Then he started choosing some things that were not good. The other one stayed in church and Sunday School and tried to do what was right." The prisoner continued, "It has been years since that time and I am here to tell you that both of those boys are here in this prison tonight. The one who tried to do right is the one who is going to preach to you in a few minutes. The one who thought he was smart and chose to do wrong is this prisoner who is introducing him to you."[4]

Two boys, both with the freedom to choose, and it's us, too. We have the freedom to choose what we will do with our lives. Will it be a happy New Year? It depends on the choices we make. In spite of what happens to any of us in the year ahead, it can be a very happy, blessed, good year if we will choose every day of it to serve the Lord. But it is our choice. It's in our hands. What will we do?

Notes

1. *Pulpit Resource* (January, February, March 1983), 29.

2. Christian Commentator's Library, "How Old Are You?" n.d., 10-11.

3. Robert McCracken, *Putting Faith to Work,* (New York: Harper & Brothers, 1960), 148.

4. Hardy R. Denham, Jr., "Getting Ready for Easter," *Proclaim* (January, February, March 1984): 7.

2
Valentine's Day:
Are You in Love?

(with Jesus?)

I'm going to take my life in my hands because I'm going to talk about love. Whenever you do that, you run the danger of somebody telling you that you don't know what you're talking about. That may be true. Do any of us know what we're talking about? When we talk about love, how would you define it? I imagine we would get as many definitions as there are people. *Love* is a word that has been abused, misused, and confused. It has been used to describe everything from the crudest pornography all the way to Christ's crucifixion. How would you define love?

While we might not be able to define it, I think we can certainly see what love does. If somebody tells you that they love you, how do you know? You will know by the way they treat you. Love is seen in deeds. This is what the Bible seeks to tell us. In the Bible, the word *love* is usually a verb, not a noun. It's a call to action. "Love . . . as I have loved you" (John 13:34). "Beloved, let us love one another" (1 John 4:7). "God so loved the world that he gave" (John 3:16). "Love your neighbor" (Matt. 19:19). "Love your enemies" (Luke 6:27). You soon get the idea that love is something that you do.

As we think of this Valentine's Day, I want to ask you a question: Are you in love? Most of us would say yes. We've been married for a long time, or we have a sweetheart, surely we are in love. How do we know? How can we tell whether we are in love or not? It will be seen in what we do and what is it that we have to do in order to know that we are in love?

To answer that, I want to use the example of the highest expression of love we can think about—Christ. He has shown us love like no one else can or ever did or ever will. To understand what love does, we need to see how Christ lived. There are three characteristics we need to have if love is ours.

I. If we are in love, we are unselfish.

When Christ came, He came to die for us. When God created the world, He gave us everything we needed for a good life, but we didn't want to live by His terms. We rebelled against Him and erected a barrier between God and ourselves, and we couldn't climb over it. Life was squeeaed out of us—the joy, the celebration, the love. But God still tried to show us love. Through prophets and priests, He tried to reach us. Finally, He came in Christ to undo what we had done. Christ came to do something for us, not for Himself. When He died on the cross, He did not die for anything He had done, but for everything we had done. He gave us what we did not deserve—a love we didn't deserve, a forgiveness we didn't deserve, and a hope we didn't deserve. He gave it because He loved us, and His love was expressed by thinking of us first, not of Himself. This is a characteristic of true love, it thinks of the other first. True love asks: "What can I do for you?" not "What can you do for me?" True love has the highest good of the other as its concern. It doesn't say, "Please me," it says, "What can I do to please you?"

Tragically, most of the time our love is selfish. We think of ourselves first and not of the needs of others. There was a boy who was put in a counseling center in Richmond, Virginia at eight years of age. He got into fights with others, didn't want to go to school, and threw rocks at passing cars. On his birthday, his mother, a very rich lady, came to visit the boy and bought him a very expensive camera. The boy was very excited at getting the camera and ran over to give his mother a hug. She said, "Don't touch me, you might rumple my dress." The counselor said, "The mother left with her dress not rumpled, but in a very short time, that expensive camera was smashed to bits."[1]

Why? The boy needed love, but she was interested in not wrinkling her dress. Selfishness: my needs first, not yours! Too often this is the kind of love we settle for. You can hear it in some of the expressions people say: "You don't make me happy anymore," saying that what the other persons were there to do was to make them happy. The truth is: it's the other way around. You are there to make the other person happy. Or someone says to another, "If you love me, you will go all the way." That's one of the biggest lies that one will ever hear because if a person loves you, he will never want you to go against your highest good, to go against what is best for you, never want you to go against your highest principles. Or someone in marriage says, "I have my rights." Yes, you do have your rights, but don't you understand that when you get married, you give up your personal rights for the rights of the marriage?

In the movie *Serenade,* a man named Damon Vincent worked in a vineyard. A very rich socialite named Mrs. Hale found him and made a singer out of him, but she possessed and dominated him. He was like one of her masks, someone who belonged to her. The theory she had was that whatever was good for her was what Damon Vincent must do. Eventually, it squeezed the life out of him, and he ran away from his career to Mexico to lose himself because he was so unhappy. There he met a daughter of a Mexican rancher who loved him, who cared for him; her philosophy was this: "Whatever is good for Damon, that is my concern." That kind of love rescued Damon and brought him back from despair to hope and to life again. "Whatever is good for Damon, that is my concern."[2]

In your marriage, is this what you say? "Whatever is good for the one I'm married to, that is my concern." Those other relationships that you call love, is this your concern, whatever is good for the other matters most? We're in love if our love is unselfish.

II. If we are in love, our love is accepting in hope.

What impresses me about the love of Christ is that we didn't have to be perfect to get it. It would have been bad if we had to have been perfect. Imagine Him coming to Matthew, that dishonest tax collector, and telling him, "You've got to clean up your dishonesty, and then you can come follow Me." Do you think Matthew would have done that? Or go to that fisherman, impetuous Peter, who cussed like a fisherman. If Jesus had said to him, "Clean up your language, and then you can follow Me," do you think Peter would have done it? Or to John, that "son of thunder" who lost his temper just like that, if Jesus had said, "Clean up your temper, then you can follow Me." Do you think John would have done it? I doubt it.

But Jesus did not come with a finger of judgement; He came instead with the arms of acceptance and love. He loved them into becoming more than they were and, because He loved them and cared for them, He was able to turn Matthew from his dishonesty into a diligent for Him; to turn John, the "son of thunder," into one known as "the apostle of love." Why? Because Christ accepted them and loved them.

Often we have it the other way around. We tell people, "If you believe like I believe, then you can be my brother in Christ." Or, "If you cut your hair or shine your shoes, then I will like you." Or, "If you will be what I want you to be and make good grades, then I'll be proud of you." We give the message to people that they are not accepted, and this must not be. This is not love. Love does not come with a pointed finger of judgment, but with accepting arms of love that reaches out and hugs people to themselves and in love, believes that they are more than what seems to be on the surface.

It's like the classic story of beauty and the beast. The poor farmer's daughter had to live with this half-man, half-beast-looking creature as a punishment in order to keep her father out of jail for a robbery he had committed. The monster fell in love with her and asked her over and over again to marry him, but she could not do it. Finally, he became weaker and weaker and seemed to be dying. He asked her one more time if she would marry him, and this time she had a change of heart and said yes. She leaned over and kissed that hideous face. The face disappeared, and there was a handsome prince charming who had been under a curse and had to stay under the curse until he could find someone who would love him, not for what he looked like but for what he was.[3]

All of us sometimes look like a beast on the outside. What we need are those who can see our beauty on the inside, those who know that there is more than meets the eye and who will believe in us, accept us, and in love inspire us to be something more. I am thankful to God that He did not judge us by what He has seen on the outside but what He knows that we can be with His help. Love reaches out to people in hope, loving people to higher heights, believing in people, inspiring them to something more.

Somerset Maughan once described the Russian novelist, Dostoevsky, as "vain, envious, quarrelsome, suspicious, cringing, selfish, boastful, unreliable, inconsiderate, narrow, and intolerant . . . But," he added, "this is not the whole story."[4]

Love knows that what one sees is "not the whole story." There's more to us!

III. We are in love if our love stays, whatever.

Christ loved us and suffered for it: ridicule and rejection, pain and persecution, death. And His love didn't seem to do any good. The crowds left Him, Peter denied Him, and Judas betrayed Him. All He did was love, and nobody seemed to get the message or care. But He did not stop loving us. He hung on the cross and suffered all of that to let us know how much He did care. His love would not quit even though it was treated badly, often rejected, and even ignored. His love still came. The quality of the love of Christ is that it will never stop, it goes on and on forever. No matter what we do to reject it, laugh at it, ignore it, run from it, or crucify it, it still comes. It's a love that's committed for an eternity.

The quality of love is that it never ends. It ought to be true, like that commitment we make at the marriage altar—for better, for worse, for richer, for poorer, in sickness and in health, till death do us part. That is a commitment that your love is real, and no matter what happens, it will stay. A couple was very much in love before the Civil War, but the war separated them. He had to go fight, but he wrote every day. One day a letter didn't come. After a few days, a letter did come, and in it he said, "My dearest, I'm having a friend write this because in the last battle, I lost both arms and now somebody is going to have to wait on me for the rest of my life. I love you too much to ask that of you, so I'm releasing you from our engagement." When she got the letter, she immediately packed and went to that hospital. She walked down to that bed where he was lying, threw her arms around his neck and kissed him, and said, "These hands will always take care of you. I will never, never let you go. For you see, I love you."[5]

Love doesn't stop when the difficult comes. Love doesn't stop when the suffering comes. Love doesn't stop when the problems arise. Instead, love tackles them head-on. You just don't quit. You work it out. You don't run, you stay with it. Someone has defined love as "something you've been through with somebody." Love can go through anything if we've committed ourselves to true love. It will not stop.

So the question: Are you in love? Are you in love to the place where your love is unselfish, that what the other person wants is more important than what you want? Are you so much in love that you accept one another in hope? Are you so much in love that you will never quit loving, no matter how difficult or hard it may seem to be.

   That's a high call to love. Unfortunately, most of the time we settle for less, for cheaper imitations of love. Here's the truth. We cannot love like I have described unless the love of Christ dwells in us. We have to abide in Him in order for this love to be possible in our lives. The more in love we are with Christ, the more we will be able to love one another. The more we are committed to the Christ of love, the more we will find ourselves loving one another in the way that we ought. If we want our marriages to be better, what we need to do first is to get our commitment to Christ stronger. If we want our lives to be better, what we need to do is get our commitment to Christ better. If we want life to be what it ought to be, what we've got to do is to give ourselves to the giver of life. We cannot be what we ought to be and love as we ought to love until Christ lives in us.

   Does He? The first question is this: Are we in love with Christ? If we are in love with Christ, then we will be able to love one another in the way that we ought to love one another. That sounds simple, but it is the toughest commitment we will ever make, to love Christ with our hearts and souls and minds and everything that is within us. But remember, if we make that tough commitment, it will bring us the greatest joy we can ever know, for we will be consumed by love for one another that is precious, sweet, and unending!

Notes

   1. John Redhead, "The Needs of Childhood," *The Protestant Hour* (26 February-2 April 1967): 5.

   2. Charles A. McClain, Jr., "Do You Have 'Charisma?' " *Pulpit Preaching* (May-June 1972): 7.

   3. John R. Claypool, "The Creative Power of Love," Sermon: Crescent Hill Baptist Church, Louisville, Kentucky, 12 September 1971, 1-2.

   4. James Armstrong, *The Journey the Men Make* (Nashville: Abingdon Press, 1969), 87.

   5. James S. Flora, "When Two Become One," *The New Pulpit Digest* (May-June 1973): 13.

3
Baccalaureate Sermon:
Earning a Passing Grade

(Matt. 19:16-22)

Many years ago I heard Charles Fuller, the pastor of the First Baptist Church, Roanoke, preach a sermon at the University of Richmond, Virginia. It was entitled: "The 'A' Student Who Failed." It was based upon this text of the rich young ruler. I don't remember too much about the sermon, but I do remember thinking at the time that it would be a good subject for a baccalaureate sermon or a commencement address: the story of a rich young ruler who had made it big in the eyes of the world, but who was a failure in the eyes of God. So I put it on file in my memory, to be recalled that day when I would be asked to give a baccalaureate address or to preach a commencement sermon.

Well, I'm still waiting. Every now and then the horrible thought occurs to me that I may never be asked to do such a thing. So on this Sunday when we honor those who are graduating in our church fellowship, I thought it would be a good time to make believe and pretend that I have been asked to give such a sermon. That's what I'm going to do, to try to write a word to those who have graduated from any school and who are now attempting to make their way through life.

But it is also a word for any of us at any time. It's about the process of trying to earn a passing grade at the important thing in the world: making a life. Here we had a young ruler, rich, successful in the eyes of the world, a man of authority. He was a good man, a man who had kept many of the Commandments from his youth up: successful, rich, decent. If there ever was a man who seemed to have it made, he was that man. A success, "grade *A*" style. But yet, not so! He wanted to know what he needed to do to gain eternal life, and Jesus told him. There's one thing he lacked. It was a big thing. It was a matter of commitment to values, a matter of what he believed was first and foremost in his life. I want to talk about our need to earn a passing mark in trying to make a life worth living.

I. To earn a passing mark in making a life, we need to remember that people and our relationships with them are more important than possessions or things.

Evidently, this young ruler had placed a lot of faith in his possessions. He had great possessions, but they were getting in the way of his commitment to Christ and to everything that had lasting value. Jesus brought him face-to-face with that conflict. "Go, sell what you possess and give to the poor, . . . come, follow me" (v. 21). Give them up for a relationship with Christ and with the rest of the disciples. Become more concerned and compassionate about the poor and needy. Remember that relationships with real live people are more important than relationships with things, power, and prestige. But he couldn't do it! He could not give up his possessions.

This is probably one of the greatest temptations we will face at any stage of life, the temptation to put people secondary to possessions, prestige, or power. There's a lot of rhetoric being uttered from commencement pulpits these days saying that young people must go out and make their mark in life. Often we interpret making our mark as making a lot of money, being tops in our careers, or surrounding ourselves with many of the material comforts of life. We have been taught to believe that's where life is. To have all of these material possessions is to be full of life. But what Jesus has been trying to tell us is that it's not so. The most important resource we have in life is people. The secret of life is to develop meaningful relationships with one another, to share with each other, to commit ourselves to one another, to realize that people are the source of our joy.

If we listen to others long enough, if we read long enough, we should hear it! However, I'm not sure we believe it. Arthur Miller wrote a book entitled *The Price,* a story of two brothers. One of them was named Walter. He was a brilliant surgeon who had all of the things that the world considered successful, but as he was talking with his brother toward the end of his days, he talked about a breakdown he had experienced. He said his breakdown was caused by a fanatic determination to be the best, and to be the best "you eliminate everything extraneous, including people. You become a kind of instrument, an instrument that cuts money out of people, or fame out of the world. . . . You get to thinking that because you frighten people, they love you. I wanted to be tops but I ended up in a swamp of success and bankbooks. . . . It adds up to a life governed by the ambition to get things for oneself instead of doing things for others."[1]

People have told us over and over again that when we get to the top, it feels empty and lonely. A television play called "The Failure" was a story of a man who had a minor position in a bank. He didn't make too much money, which was an inconvenience for his family. All the other people in the neighborhood and the friends of this man's children seemed to have a lot more things. The children didn't like it, and one day he overheard his teenage daughter say to his wife, "Daddy's a failure, isn't he?"

A failure? A man who was faithful to his wife for years, a man who worked decently and honestly in his work with integrity, a man who gave up a chance at a promotion in the bank to attend his daughter's graduation? Is such a man a failure? As the play progressed, one began to get the feeling that one day these children might understand what blessings they had, that they would be able to look back and discover where it counted—in the learning of love, of faithfulness, of integrity—the father was not a failure at all, but quite a success.[2]

People are important. Friendships are most important. If you ever want to find life, you've got to find it in developing relationships with people.

II. To earn a passing mark in making a living, we need to be willing to risk ourselves for that which is highest and best.

What Jesus was asking of the rich young ruler was quite a risk—to give away all his possessions and to follow an itinerant preacher to who knows where. Quite a risk! He had security. He was well respected in his community, and Jesus was saying, "Throw all that away. Take a chance on Me. Risk it for what you believe might be the best and the highest." And the young man wouldn't do it. We would have thought he was crazy if he did, wouldn't we? To leave all of that behind to follow Jesus. But the man never would know whether the risk would have been worth it. Since he wasn't willing to take the dare, he didn't discover the joy of eternal life.

Life is full of risks. We will have to choose to live it by risk or by playing it safe. We've got to choose which values are worth it, which values will bring us life. Then we've got to take a chance on those values we say we believe in. We believe love is more important than hate! Will we risk ourselves for love? Will we forgive people? Will we accept people? Will we risk ourselves for love knowing that we might not be loved back, and it's painful when we're not. But there is pain in not loving. Being lonely is a pain. Not knowing the joy of what love can bring is pain. We've got to risk it for love. Are we willing to risk it?

We say that peace is better than war. We all believe that. It seems we've done a lot to ensure peace by building more and bigger nuclear weapons that can wipe us out in the push of a button. I wonder if anyone is willing to risk being a peacemaker in these days, to rise up and say, "No more. We have enough of that. Let's quit trying to retaliate against each other and start negotiating with one another." It's risky. Do we believe in peace enough to risk for it?

We say right is better than wrong. We believe in right, but are we willing to risk ourselves for it? To risk a life of being honest, to risk a life of being morally pure, to risk trying to discover and get equal rights for everyone? Are we willing to risk the fight against injustice of any kind, against prejudice in any shape and form, and against narrow-minded people who only look out for themselves?

Are we willing to risk it rather than play it safe? There are no guarantees that when we risk, we will not be wounded. Jesus risked Himself and got crucified. But He was a man who knew how to live, and if we're going to find life, we've got to be willing to risk ourselves for the highest and the best.

Let me share this with young people. There was a time when we "older folks" were willing to risk, too. We had our dreams. We knew that there were dragons out there waiting for us, but we were going to go out and slay them in order to make the world a better place. But as we got out there and started struggling with them, some of those dragons were big and menacing looking, and they breathed fire that hurt. Unfortunately, some of us got tired of fighting them and wondered if it was worth it. Often, we quit. That is why the world is not what it ought to be. The dragons are out there for you. They will try to hurt you. They will resist you, but please, risk yourself to fight them. Try to slay them. Try to make this world a better place than when you found it. We need you to do that. Less than that is to cheat yourself of the adventure of life.

Two men graduated from the Royal Naval Academy and were given commissions in the British navy. One chose not to accept it. Instead, he chose to live his life being a shrimp-boat captain on the Thames River. He felt there was more security in that. The other became an officer in the navy, sailed the seas, and became a very famous officer. He became an admiral. He conquered Napoleon's fleet and earned great fame. Nelson was his name. Some years later, Nelson was standing on that dock by the shrimp boat with his friend and classmate. He looked at the boat and then looked at the Atlantic Ocean stretching out there. With tears in his eyes, Nelson said to his friend, "You could have had all that," then looking at the shrimp boat, he added, "but you settled for this."[3]

Don't settle for less than the best. Life is found in risking yourself, not playing it safe but playing it sacrificially.

III. To earn a passing mark in life, we need to be willing to trust Christ.

This is what Jesus told the rich young man: "You want eternal life, here's what you've got to do. Put Me first. Trust Me. Believe I know the way. Follow Me. Then you'll find it." But the young man didn't do it. He didn't do it because possessions were first with him rather than Christ.

This is the challenge that all of us have in life, and you expect me to say it because I'm a preacher. You expect me to say that to find life, you've got to follow Christ. I do say it. To find life abundant and eternal, you need to follow Christ. I say it because I believe it. I believed it before I became a preacher, and I stay a preacher because I believe it still. All of us have to have some guide to follow. All of us have to have some center around which we order our lives, and the best center is the God we have discovered in Christ. He made us. He knows best how we can live. We need to trust Him for it. There will always be false gods trying to take the throne of our lives, and they will always fail us. Only God will bring us life if we have faith enough to trust Him.

Christ answers our questions. Who are we? We are His children created in His image, and that is good. Why are we here? We are here to serve Him, to do His will. That means to make the world a better place, to help people become better than they are. How can we do it? By the power of His grace. We cannot succeed on our own resources alone, but through His love and grace and forgiveness. Where does it all end? It ends in the kingdom of God where everything we've done for His sake will last, where everyone of us who loves Him will celebrate forever the joy of His kingdom.

Now I can't make you believe that. I can't argue you into that. I can't convince you beyond a shadow of an intellectual doubt that this is the way to go. You've got to take a risk for that, too. You've got to decide. Is Christ the Lord? Can you trust Him or not? What the Scripture tells us and what millions down through the years have told us is that, when we trust Him, we will find life.

A man wrote about lying in no-man's land on the battlefield. He had been wounded. He needed help. In the distance, he heard someone coming and saw a shadowy figure. He could not make the figure out. Was it a friend or foe? If he yelled out, would he get a helping hand or a bullet? But he needed help desperately, and he had to make the decision in that moment. Which would he do? Finally, he cast his lot and cried out, "Who goes there?" It turned out to be a friend who reached out a helping hand, bound his wounds, and brought him to life.[4]

Many shadowy figures walk in our lives, coming toward us calling for our allegiance. We cry out, "Who goes there?" But there's only One who will reach down to bind our wounds and give us life. Christ is always waiting to be called, always waiting to reach out. If we want to have life, we need to live it His way. We need to follow Him.

We do congratulate our graduates. This is a significant milestone in their lives, but it is only a foothold that ought to lead you to more. Remember one of the root words of graduation is the word *gradual.* That is an indication of what education is. It's a gradual thing. When do you finally get it? When you're no longer here. Whenever you stop learning, you stop living. If you really want to know how to make a life and how to get the most out of it, here's what you need to do. Major on people and relationships with them. They are more important than all of the things you can hold in your hands. Be willing to take a risk for that which is right and the best. Don't settle for less than the best. Pay whatever price necessary to reach it. Trust Christ along the way. However difficult and hard it may be, never lose hold on Him. He will never let you down.

What I would say to you who are graduating is what they said of the man who was a mountain climber. On one of his mountain climbs, the rock broke the rope, and the man fell to his death. His friends buried him right where he fell and put these words on his tombstone, "He died climbing."[5] I hope all of us will *live* climbing.

Notes

1. C. Thomas Hilton, "If I Had My Life to Live Over," *The Clergy Journal* (January 1981), 10.

2. Leonard Griffeth, *Illusions of Our Culture* (Waco, Tex.: Word Books, 1969), 114-115.

3. James Buckingham, "Missing the Mark," *Survey* (December 1962), 26.

4. J. Wallace Hamilton, *Who Goes There?* (Westwood, N.J.: Fleming H. Revell Company, 1958), 11-12.

5. Gaston Foote, *Living in Four Dimensions* (Westwood, N.J.: Fleming H. Revell Company, 1953), 47-48.

4
Children's Day:
The Child We Need to Be

(Luke 18:15-17)

Every Mother's Day and Father's Day, my children say to me that they ought to set aside a day in the year for children: a Children's Day. Probably when your children told you the same thing, you replied as I did, "Every day is Children's Day. We provide for you all the time. We try to take care of you all the time. Every day is your day. You don't need a special day." But for all those children who wanted to have a Children's Day, I've got news for you. On the national calendar, a day has been designated as Children's Day, a day to celebrate the gift of children and to be thankful for them.

Indeed we are. Children are special and precious gifts from God, and we need to celebrate them. As we come on this Children's Day, I call our attention to this particular passage where Jesus said that unless we become like children, we cannot be part of the kingdom of God. (v. 17) Every one of us who wants to be part of God's kingdom needs to be like a child. When I first read that, it bothered me. There are a lot of things about children that are not exactly admirable. They have a lot of qualities and traits that don't seem to be positive. Sometimes they are very selfish; all they are interested in is their own way. Often they are petty and picky, jealous of one another. Often they do not want to shoulder responsibility, letting others do it for them. Sometimes they are violent, thinking the only way to solve problems is through a fist on the jaw. Surely Jesus wasn't talking about that, was He? When

He wanted us to become like children, He was not asking for those qualities, was He?

I hope not. We need to notice there is a difference between "childishness" and "childlikeness." There are certain qualities we can have that are childish and immature. When an adult shows these qualities, we call them "childish." Sadly, I have known many adults who showed the childish qualities just mentioned. Many adults are selfish; all they are concerned about is what *they* want out of life. Many adults are picky, petty, and jealous of others. That is often the root of gossip. Many adults will not shoulder the responsibility of life. They will not accept the responsibility of being their own person and making their own decisions. Many adults think that the only solution to problems is violence and anger. That's childishness. Christ wants us to have no part of that.

Instead, He wants us to be childlike, to have some of the attitudes that a child has when she was young, when she came into life pure and innocent. Some of these same qualities and attitudes are needed as we make our way through the kingdom of God.

I. We need to have an attitude of openness to life, seeing life as an adventure to experience, not just a time to endure.

The children were coming to listen to Jesus and the disciples were trying to keep them away from Him. "He is too busy for you." Jesus said, "Not so. Let them come. I enjoy their presence." Jesus enjoyed the curiosity of children. They wanted to come see who He was. They wanted to come listen to Him. They probably wanted to come just to touch Him. Jesus said, "Let them come. I want them to."

Some years ago, Johnny Cash made a film called *Gospel Road.* The life of Christ was depicted and one of the memorable scenes in it was of Christ and children playing with each other on the beach. They were romping around, having a real good time. What made it memorable was that such is not the image we have of Christ. Often the image we have of Christ is that He is stern, aloof, somewhat of a sourpuss-type person. You just can't enjoy being around Him. God is not so at all! Children love to be in the presence of Christ, and I know for a fact that children don't love to be in the presence of a grouch. They love to play with people, and Jesus loved to play with them. They were curious about Him, and Jesus allowed their curiosity. Life was an adventure and an exciting thing to experience, and Jesus encouraged it.

Children are that way. As soon as a child learns to crawl, nothing in the house is safe. Everything can be destroyed, and we work to try to make our house childproof against them, but it never works. Children do that, not because they want to destroy but because they are so interested in finding out what is going on. Life is a big thrill for them, something new to experience every moment and every day. That is why they are into everything. Look at a child when you take him to the circus for the first time. Watch his eyes and see them bug wide open at each new exciting experience to see. Then look at us, years later, going through life more content with the familiar than the unfamiliar. One of the problems of maturity is: the older we get, the less life becomes an adventure and more a time to endure. We don't look upon each new day as something new and exciting—a gift from God—with so much that can be seen in it. We rush through life and never see it.

> Jules Feiffer, a cartoonist with a serious intent, has an eight-panel cartoon that shows a person from boyhood to maturity, resisting every change, every transition. When they dragged me to school at five, I remember screaming: "But I'm not ready!" When they sent me to summer camp at ten, I remember screaming: "But I'm not ready!" When they drafted me at nineteen, I remember screaming: "But I'm not ready!" When they married me off at twenty-three, I remember screaming: "But I'm not ready!" When they made me a father at 24, 25, and 26, I remember screaming: "But I'm not ready!" The last panel in the series shows a grown man, hiding in a hole in the ground and saying: "Finally, at fifty, I ran away from my wife, and kids, and my grandchildren . . . and I'm not coming out again until I'm ready."[1]

Most of us go through life never ready to face it. We rebel against it, not ready to enjoy it. What we need to realize is that each new day is an exciting adventure, and there is no telling, since God is in it, what each new day can bring us. Instead of living life bored, we ought to live life with excitement. We ought to be sensitive to all the sounds, the smells, the colors, and experiences of it. Too many of us never get anything out of life because we lose our sense of adventure and excitement.

I ran across some words that somebody had written thinking over his past life. He wrote these words that maybe you have heard. "If I had my life to live over, I would try to make more mistakes. I would relax. I would be sillier than I have been this trip. I would be less hygenic. I would go more places, climb more mountains, swim more rivers. I would eat more ice cream and less spinach. I would have more actual troubles and less imaginary ones. You see, I have been one of those fellows who lived prudently, hour after hour, day after day. Oh, I have had my moments. But if I had to do it all over again, I would have more of them, a lot more. I never go anywhere without a thermometer, a raincoat, or a parachute. If I had to do it over, I would travel much lighter. If I had my life to live over, I would start going barefoot a little earlier in the spring and stay that way a little later in the fall. I would have more dogs. I would sleep later hours. I would have more sweethearts. I would fish more. I would ride more merry-go-rounds. I would go to more circuses. If I had my life to live over, I would pick more daisies."[2]

It's sad sometimes that when we come to the end of our lives, we look back over them and say, "If only I had done this." Life is here for us now. Each day can be something new and exciting if we are sensitive to it, and if, when we wake up in the morning, we thank God for what is coming about. I like the spirit of the child who was asked one time, "Can you play the piano?" she said, "I don't know. I have never tried it." There is no telling what we can get out of life if we put more into it and look at it with excitement and live on tiptoe with our eyes wide open at the wonders that God has given to us each moment.

II. We need to have an attitude of dependency.

A child was not afraid to go to Jesus, not afraid to play with Him, not afraid to talk with Him, not afraid to be with Him. A child is not afraid of others early. He learns very early in life that he needs others for survival. He depends on them for food, clothes, and shelter, for love and security. Children grow up needing other people. One of the constant cries of young children is, "Help me. Help me tie my shoes. Help me build a sand castle. Help me ride a bike. Help me walk a mile. Play with me. Do something with me." They want to be with people. They are willing to depend on others. They are so dependent on others for life. They don't crawl into a shell and say, "I don't need you."

Unfortunately, the older we get, the more we hear the message, "You don't need others. You can make it on your own." One boy grew up hearing: you have to be a success; you have to look out for number one. If you don't look out for yourself, who will? Don't trust anybody. Stand on your own two feet. So he did and sought to be a business executive. He kept that in mind, doing only what was best for him, needing no one, stepping on people's backs as he climbed up the ladder. Finally, he got to the top. He was a self-made man. He needed no one. That's how many friends he had. He didn't care for anybody, only for himself. How many of us do that? How many of us feel that we are self-sufficient, don't need anybody, and can handle everything on our own?

There was a young woman I knew once who had gone through a terrible crisis. She had quit coming to church. She said simply, "When I get my troubles straightened out, then I will be back." I asked, "Why then? For church is where we share our troubles and burdens, and together we get through things. Why wait?" "No, I had rather do it alone." How sad, when we carry our burdens all by ourselves.

A college professor said, "Throw away the crutch. You don't need God anymore. When you were young, maybe you needed this image to keep you going, to give you a sense of security. But now you have outgrown that idea of God, that need of God. You don't need Him anymore." Many of us grow up in the church and go to Sunday School, and all is well and good. Then we become junior-high and senior-high people, and we hear it, "We don't need God. We don't need church." Many drop out during that time.

Many in our day are having the same struggles. They need no one. It is one of the tragic mistakes in life to think that you can live it, independent of others. All the way through the Bible, God tried to get us that message: "Am I my brother's keeper?" (Gen. 4:9), the question was asked. We were meant to be: "It is not good for the man to be alone" (Gen. 2:18, NASB). "Love your neighbor" (Matt. 5:43). What better thing can a man do than to lay down his life for his friends" (John 15:13, author paraphrase)? All the way through, the Bible is hollering at us: "We need each other." We were meant to live life with one another. We can't be alone and know what it is to experience the joy of life. Life was not made that way. A lot of us would be helped if we would quit going through life feeling that we can handle everything on our own. We box ourselves up in a shell and hide from one another, never giving ourselves away to one another. Life was never meant to be that way. Like a child who easily runs up to hug you, a child who finds it easier to say "I love you" than adults do, we need each other. If we don't depend on one another, one day we will come up empty, short, and alone.

A boy went to camp. As he got off the bus, he acted tough. He knew how to make his bed, he knew how to organize his materials. He didn't need anybody to tell him anything. In fact, the boy spent his afternoon telling others, "You need to do this, you need to do that. I know how to do that. Listen to me, and I will tell you." He didn't need anybody. That night as the counselor slept in bed, all of a sudden something pounced in that bed and with a hammer-lock, grabbed the neck of that boy who had been so self-sufficient, so sure of himself. He didn't need anybody to tell him anything or do anything for him. But that boy was shivering and afraid, because of what? Because of the sound of beetles chirping in the night.[3] All of us may act tough, all of us may act like we don't need anybody, but deep down inside, behind all that tough exterior, is a heart made for other people, a heart meant to reach out and commit oneself and risk oneself to love. We would get a whole lot more out of life if we would go through life saying to one another, "I need you."

III. We need to have an attitude of trust.

Children were not afraid of Christ. They did not run from Him. They ran to Him. There was something about Him that caused them not to fear but to trust.

Early in life, your children trust you as parents. If you put them on a table or a stair and say to them, "Jump," without hesitation they jump and you catch them. There is not a question: "Should I really trust my father or my mother?" They don't doubt it. They just do it. They believe you are trustworthy.

They will grow up with trust if we prove trustworthy. Psychologists and psychiatrists tell us that the most crucial years in the life of children are the first two years. If their needs are met during those two years, if they learn security and love, then it will be a whole lot easier for them to trust people as they grow older. It is a shame that the older we get the less trusting we become. Some of it is necessary. We need to be doubtful of some things and some people. I am not calling for blind, naive trust. We live in an imperfect world with imperfect people, some who are not worthy of trust. But yet, when we think about trust, we've got to have somebody or something to trust. Will we trust God or ourselves? Will we trust God or money? Will we trust God or pleasure? Who will we trust to bring us life? Who promises it? Who seems to have the key to it?

I present to you—Christ. If you are talking about someone to trust, here is Someone who has been trustworthy. Here is Someone who came down to this earth, to walk where we walk, to live and face what we face, to suffer what we suffer. He climbed the cross and died, not because of anything He had done but because of everything we had done. He died for *our* sins. Then He rose, to once again tell us that His love cannot be conquered, His kingdom is forever, and if we put our trust in Him, He will never betray us. That's what He has done for us. We have to make the decision whether or not what He has done for us is more than what others have done for us. Money will never do that. Pleasure will never do that. Popularity will never do that. While we know people who mean much to us, they have never gone that far for us and never can. Christ is the One who is working for us. Christ is the One who is trustworthy.

Children grow up early believing in God without too much difficulty. Christ was saying that we need to have that simplicity of faith. Not simple faith but simplicity of faith, the kind that trusts God because He is trustworthy, that believes that whatever comes, He is the key to life. For He is! If we are ever going to know the joy of any kind of life at all, we have got to start and center it around Him.

There's a picture of a man in a little skiff out in the middle of the night. There is a storm brewing. The waves are kicking up around the little boat, and the man is rowing his way back to shore. Up in the dark sky through a little cloud is a star, one star to guide him. He stares and keeps his eye on that star as he rows his way to safety. At the bottom of the painting are the words, "If I lose that, I am lost."

Christ has come to be the star for all the darkness and all the storms of life, to guide us through them. If we ever take our eyes away from Him, we do become lost and struggle with emptiness, misery, and pain. To keep our eyes on Him is to be found.

A child's trust must become an adult's faith. There was a man who claimed to be an atheist. He believed there was no use believing. In his childhood, he said his father had put him on a high table and said, "Jump, I'll catch you." The child jumped, and when he did, the father stepped back and let him hit the floor. He said to him, "That is the way life is, boy. The sooner you learn it, the better."

That's a lie! It's a lie because God is a Father who will never let us fall that way. If we live life with openness and excitement, dependency on one another, and faith and trust in God, whenever we jump anywhere, we jump into His arms. Whenever He holds us, we are held forever. No matter how old we get, I hope we'll always have a faith like a child, to believe now and forever that Christ is a Father we can trust with our lives. We can, and we must!

Notes

1. Culver Nelson, "Saul: Will the Foundation Hold?" *Master Sermons,* March 1983, 117-118.

2. Thomas L. Jones, "If I Had It to Do Over Again," *The 1978 Presbyterian Series of the Protestant Hour,* 9.

5
Memorial Day:
The Sacrifice We Must Make

(Rom. 5:1-2)

Not too long ago in Washington, D.C., a wall was built and on it were inscribed the names of the thousands who had died in the Vietnam War, perhaps the most controversial war in our nation's history. Our participation in that war and the value of it is still being debated. But whatever our opinions, that wall is very symbolic, for it reminds us that thousands of people sacrificed their lives in that distant country. Most of them were young people who wanted to hold on to life. Their names are on that wall. All of us owe them a great debt. Down through the years in many wars, millions have sacrificed their lives for the causes of freedom, brotherhood, and for their country. On this Memorial Day weekend, we must remember their sacrifice and thank God for their precious gift.

As we go to church, we also must remember another sacrifice. The sacrifice of Christ on the cross brought the greatest hope and freedom to the world. His sacrifice was a struggle to make. In the darkness of Gethsemane, He wrestled with whether He wanted to do it, but when He left there, He was willing to climb the cross to die for you and me. That's the greatest sacrifice anyone has ever made for us. But why? Why must we always remember it? This was what Paul was talking about in the Scripture. Out of his experiences, he shared the reason we must never forget Christ's sacrifice. Paul reminded us of what it did for us.

I. It was a sacrifice that brought us peace with God.

"We have peace with God through our Lord Jesus Christ" (v. 1). This means that before the cross there was a war going on, a war between God and human beings. It was a sad tale to tell. God created the world and mankind, giving them everything they needed for a good life. All they had to do was to love God and follow His guidelines. They didn't want to do that. Mankind didn't trust God. They didn't think God knew what was best for them, so they did their own thing and brought what we call "sin" into the world. The best way to remember the meaning of that word is to capitalize the *I* in the middle of it. Sin simply means doing what *I* want, not what God wants. People brought sin into the world, and when they did a wall was built between God and humans. No longer were they in fellowship and in harmony with one another. They were separated; their relationship was broken. One of the results was people began to think of God not as a friend, but as an enemy. God was somebody who had to be pleased, somebody to be feared, not loved. They established a lot of rituals and sacrifices to try to please God, to get Him on their side. They thought of God as a Judge and not as a Redeemer.

Then Christ came to show people that God was really love and the cross was the explanation point that tried to prove it. God was not against them. He was *for* them. He was always working in history on their behalf, trying to do what was best for them. The cross was the supreme proof of it. Christ died, taking the eternal death that mankind deserved and giving them eternal life, telling them that there was no reason for war anymore. They could have peace with Him.

Often we still fight God and still have the idea that He is somehow out to get us. We can't really trust Him; we've got to watch out for Him. Sometimes the early idea we learn of God is that He is like a policeman with a nightstick, a God out to get us. When we do something wrong He's going to bash us on the head and punish us. Very early in life many of us learned to fear God, not to love Him. Sometimes in the midst of trouble and tragedy, the first words we utter are, "Why, God, did You do this to me?" as if He singled us out specifically to receive that heartbreak and that pain. It was Jesus Himself who said that the rain falls on the "just and on the unjust" (Matt. 5:45). It just happens that way. Sometimes there is no reason.

Sometimes I think we live with the idea that we've got to do certain things to please Him. We've got to go to church, be good, live and do right. If not, God will not love us anymore. So we try to earn His favor and His pleasure, never really understanding the meaning of the cross. The cross is telling us that we don't have to earn it, we've got it already. God is going to love us always, and there's nothing we can ever do to change that. God is not out to get us. God is out to redeem us, love us, and forgive us. What we need to do is realize it. We don't have to fight with God anymore; we can follow Him and know His joy and love. On the cross He ended the war and offered us peace.

A little girl was talking to her mother about wanting to become a Christian, and her mother said, "Why do you want to? What do you think it means?" She said, "Christ died on the cross for me. That is important." The mother, wanting to try to find out if she understood it, said, "Well, what do you think that meant when He died on the cross for us?" She said, "It meant that God looked down at me and said, 'You're valuable,' and then He bought me."[1]

This is what Christ did. He's looked at every one of us and told us that we are valuable to Him. He wants every one of us in His kingdom. He doesn't want to fight us. He wants to love us. Every one of us can know His love if we want to. Peace with God—no more war!

II. The sacrifice made us able to experience His presence.

That was the second point that Paul made. "Through him we have obtained access to this grace in which we stand" (v. 2). The door that shut people out from God was no longer shut. In the

Temple, they had a place called the holy of holies. This was where the presence of God dwelt and nobody could go in. A veil concealed it. The only person allowed to go in was the high priest, and he only went one time a year, on the Day of Atonement, when he made sacrifices for the people. The presence of God was cut off from the people. They couldn't go in. But when Christ died on the cross, that veil was torn in two, symbolic of the fact that nobody was ever again cut off from the presence of God. Everyone could know the benefits of God's presence—the joy, the love, and the hope. Nobody was shut out anymore. Nobody was cut off from it. Anybody could know God personally.

When Abraham Lincoln was president, one of his sons wanted to go in and see him. Lincoln was in a big meeting and his secretary said, "You can't go in and see him. He's busy." The boy said, "He's my father, and he's always got time to see me."

This is what God has for you and me. He always has time for us. We don't have to go through a priest or a preacher to get to Him. We don't have to learn a formula or repeat a prayer to get to Him. All we need is a desire to be in His presence, and there we are. This is what Christ made possible. He's torn down any doors that separate us from Him. He has taken us into the room where God dwells and said, "Here He is, we can know Him. We can know all of His blessings. We can know all of His help and strength." No longer are we cut off from God. We are right there where He is. He is right there where we are. No doors, no barriers, no walls, just freedom to be with Him.

The Royal Signal Corp has a picture that serves as their motto of a soldier, one of their own, who had gone out to repair a broken cable line. Communications had been cut off from the front lines to headquarters, and they needed it repaired. The soldier had gone out to repair it and had been killed. There his lifeless body lay with his hands connecting that cable so that the lines of communications were restored again. That picture serves as a symbol of their message and of their ministry. Underneath the picture is the one word: *Through.* He had connected the communication lines. The message could get through.[2]

That's what Christ did for us. Unfortunately, it took His death. But He reopened the line of communication between God and ourselves and every one of us now can get through to Him. There's no secret. No barrier stops it. Every one of us can talk to God and experience His presence.

III. The sacrifice made it possible to share the hope of the glory of God.

This is what Paul said, "We rejoice in our hope of sharing the glory of God" (v. 2). That means the blessings of His kingdom. God made it possible for them to be citizens of the kingdom of God with all the benefits: eternal life, love forever, joy unending, and peace that never quits. All of those benefits were available to them and nothing could stop it. The kingdom on earth may fall, but the kingdom of God will always remain. They were given the hope that, no matter what happened to them, the glory of God would reign, and they would experience it.

That is our hope, too. It is the hope that keeps us going in spite of all we have to face that is unpleasant. A lot of unwanted things happens to us in the world. Sometimes our earthly kingdoms come tumbling down. But there is one truth we live by: the kingdom of God will never come tumbling down. The peace, joy, and love we share now will be nothing compared to what we will share then. This is what the cross did. It conquered all that could stop our Kingdom from coming. It conquered sin that separated us from God. It conquered suffering that causes us agony and pain. It conquered death that seems to be the final conqueror of life. The cross led to a resurrection. The cross led to victory. It reminds us that hope of the glory of God is always possible. It's not whistling in the dark. It's hope based on what we know of Christ and believe about Him.

A young seminary student in Illinois took a train every Friday night from the seminary to his home. Late at night they would pass through a little town called Calvary, Illinois. It was called Calvary because the main thing there, in that little town, was a cemetery. At midnight, when the train made its stop, the student wondered how anybody would want to live in Calvary, with all of that death. One night, they stopped, and a man got up, pulled his coat closer up to his neck, and went out into the dark. How could he live in Calvary? What could he find there worth living for? The student watched Him as he got off and took a few steps toward that cemetery. Then he noticed something he had never seen before. On the other side in the darkness, a light turned on, a light in an apartment building that he had never noticed before. He could make out in a light the form of a woman and two children. He watched as the man stood and looked in the distance at that light, waved his hands, and started toward home. The student then realized that Calvary was not a place of death, it was a place of life, a place of hope, a place of love.[3]

Sometimes we have to go through our Calvarys on earth, with the struggles and pain that are difficult to handle, but beyond them is the light of God's kingdom, the joy of our homecoming. He made it possible. Christ's death brought the hope of His glory to us. Now there is no Calvary that symbolizes death but only a Calvary that gives us life.

On Memorial Day weekend we need to remember those who have sacrificed their lives for us. I hope we will remember and thank God for them. But we need also to remember Christ's sacrifice. He has brought us the greatest gift: freedom from death, freedom from sin, and freedom from all that would rob us of life. He has brought us His kingdom. That kingdom will never end. What I hope we will do as we remember His sacrifice is to thankfully renew our sacrifice to Him.

Corrie Ten Boom was a Christian who suffered through the concentration camps of Germany. Her faith was tested in those moments. In her book *The Hiding Place,* there is an interesting statement. She wrote,

At the unhuman prison in Germany, every Friday the Nazis made the prisoners completely undress for medical inspection. They were humiliated, especially the women having to march by grinning guards. Yet on one of those mornings, another page in The Bible let in the light for me, "He hung naked on the cross." I had not known, had not thought. The paintings, the carved crucifixion showed at least a scrap of cloth. But this, I suddenly knew, was the respect and reverence of the artists. But, oh, at the time itself, on that other Friday morning, there had been no reverence, no more than in the faces I saw around us now. I leaned toward Betsy ahead of me in the line, her shoulder blades stuck out sharp and bent beneath her skin. "Betsy," I said, "they took His clothes, too." Ahead of me I heard a gasp, "O Corrie, and I never thanked Him. I never thanked Him."[4]

Christ sacrificed Himself for us. It was not pretty, it was not easy. We must not forget it; we must always remember it. The best way to show we remember is to live sacrificially for Him.

Notes

1. James E. Hightower, Jr., comp., *Illustrating The Gospel of Matthew* (Nashville: Broadman Press, 1982), 90.

2. David A. MacLennan, *Joyous Adventure* (New York: Harper & Brothers, 1952), 114.

3. R. L. Middleton, *My Cup Runneth Over* (Nashville: Broadman Press, 1960), 17-18.

4. Corrie Ten Boom and John and Elizabeth Sherrill, *The Hiding Place* (Minneapolis, Minnesota: A Chosen Book for World Wide Pictures, 1971), 196-197.

6
July Fourth:
The Way to Freedom

(Matt. 7:13-14)

It really wasn't so long ago that Martin Luther King, in his now-famous Washington Monument speech, reminded us of the strains of the Negro spiritual that said, "Free at last, free at last, thank God Almighty, free at last." In those days King was referring to the plight of blacks as they sought to receive their freedom in this land of opportunity. But as I listen to the sounds of our world today, this is one of the words that seem to be used over and over again: "Freedom—I want it." It comes from many different places. The youth are crying that they want freedom from authority, freedom from parents, freedom to do their own thing. The oppressed minorities—Blacks, Native Americans, Latin Americans—cry out for freedom to have their fair share of life in this country. Military men cry out, "We have to have freedom, and we have to pay the price for it; we have to do anything in the world to guard against Communism. We have to be free." Some religious leaders cry out, "We want to be free, free to think and do and write what we feel is the Word of God today." From everywhere, from everyplace, comes the cry, "We want to be free."

What does it mean to be free? Each of these is crying out for freedom, but freedom means a different thing to each group. Each wants something different. But what really is freedom? How do we get it? What price do we have to pay for it? What does it mean to be "free at last"?

Somewhere along the way we hear that Christ came to set us free, to deliver us from our prisons, and here in this text, Christ deals with the way to freedom. There are two paths we can choose to travel. One is the wide path that leads to death. The other is the narrow road that leads to life. One, the wide, leads to slavery. The narrow leads to freedom, but freedom from Christ's point of view. For Christians, freedom means living up to the fullest potential for which we were made. Freedom under God means being exactly what God meant us to be. What does that really mean? How do we achieve our full potential? How do we become the people we were meant to become? Three things are implied in this text to show what true freedom is all about.

I. Freedom to become what we ought to become is an achievement; it is not a gift.

There are two roads before us. One is the narrow one not traveled by many because it's hard, lonely, and long! Then there's the wide one which everybody seems to be traveling because it's easy. Christ said, "You want life? Travel the narrow way." We don't have to. Each one of us has the freedom to choose which road we want to travel.

Here is our freedom, the freedom of choice to choose the way we will live. But once we have chosen the narrow way which leads to freedom, once we have made the choice, then we've got to walk that road. We've got to pay the consequences of our choice: the discipline, the pain, the loneliness, and maybe even the cross. One misconception we have about freedom is that we think it means we can do anything we want to do, be anything we want to be. Not so! Freedom means that we can choose what we want to do and be, but once we have made the choice, we've got to pay the price for it. The freedom to become what we want to become comes only after hard, agonizing travel down the narrow road.

For instance, you want to be a good football player. You can choose to do that, and there are two ways you can choose. You can go down the narrow way of discipline, that's the way of hours and hours of practice, of watching your diet, of observing curfew, of being willing to take the pain. Or you can take the wide way that means skipping curfew, forgetting diet, missing practices, not giving 100 percent, trying just to get by. Which way will get you what you want?

Say you want to be a lawyer or a doctor. You can choose to be that, and there are ways to get it. There is a narrow way of hard work and long hours of study, of foregoing some pleasures to conquer your tests and studies, of putting away short-range pleasures for long-range goals. Or you can try it the wide way where you miss a few classes, go to parties, and put short-range pleasures before long-range goals. Which way would get you what you want?

We want this to be a free country. OK, we can choose that, but we have to take the narrow way of responsible citizenship. We've got to know the political issues and the political candidates. We've got to exercise our rights to vote. We've got to exercise our right to make this country what it ought to be. Responsible citizenship means not saying, "My country—right or wrong," but rather, "I will work to make my country right." We can try the wide way— the way of indifference to the issues and to the candidates, the way of letting somebody else carry the load, the way of not voting, and not really caring. Which way do you think would bring us freedom?

Or we want this to be a Christian world and a Christian community. We can choose that. How do you get it? There's the narrow way of sacrifice and service; the way of dedicating ourselves to justice, and love; the way of giving to Christ our possessions and our talents; a way that is hard. Or we can take the wide way of taking Christ when it is convenient; attending church when we haven't got anything better to do; putting other things before Christ and taking Christ whenever we have the time; being indifferent, uncaring about justice and about love. We can try it that way. Which road gets it?

Freedom is not had by wishing. Freedom is only had by working. There is a price to be paid, and what bothers me is that too many people are willing to take the wide way. When Hitler came into power in the 1930s, he did not have to conquer the German people by force. Instead they were more than willing to hand over their freedom for security! "You take care of us, you give us food to eat, a place to live in, a purpose to live for, and we will sell you our souls for security!" They did! How many times are we willing to sell our souls so we won't have to travel down the narrow road? Freedom is always the result of the long hard walk.

II. True freedom comes when we are willing to base our lives on spiritual, eternal values and not on temporary, material ones.

There is a wide way that most people go. That way says, "You want freedom? Come, I'll give it to you. I know how you can get it. All you have to do is give yourself away to the physical and material and you will find freedom." We buy it, and we start traveling down the wide, easy road. But we usually discover after we have traveled down the wide road for awhile that it gets narrower, and what we thought was freedom turns out to be slavery. Take, for instance, those who tell us that, if we want to be anything in the world, we've got to be a success. That means we've got to surround ourselves with the material values of life. We've got to have things: a good home, a couple of cars, and membership in the right clubs. So we spend our lives trying to pad our bank account, trying to get things. But one day we wake up to discover we don't have things—they have us. Like a child who plays with a toy for a couple of hours and tires of it and needs a new one, so we play with our things for a while, and then we need something else: another car, another dress, another house, another what? I wonder how many of us have believed things would bring freedom and have ended up slaves to bank accounts, bills, credit cards, and debt. We have discovered the truth only too late: we cannot control things. We end up being controlled *by* them.

We can go after the other road, "Come this way. You want what? Freedom? Self-indulge. Do your own thing. Do what you want to do. Don't worry about anything else. Satisfy your physical desires." So we have. We have gone wild. We have people lost on alcohol and drugs, people miserable from satisfying their own desires. Take drugs. They promise so much. We want to expand our minds, expand our awareness, expand our lives. So we pop a pill or shoot a needle. Man, it's a good trip. Got to take another one and another one. Until one day, much to our misery, we wake up to discover that we can't live without that pill or without that needle. Who's free?

A man is proud of his freedom to eat whatever he wants to eat, and he does. He eats pork chops for breakfast, a couple of roast birds for a midnight snack, and he washes it down with a quart of orange juice. He's free, all 300-plus pounds of him. But is he? Take away his roast birds and his pork chops and see how free he is. He will go insane with hunger. He has become a prisoner to his desires. He's free to be a slave.

There is a wide way that promises much, but the truth is that one day the bills come due. When they do, they are too high.

But Christ says there's a narrow way to life: travel it. You want to know what it is? The narrow way means to *love.* That's hard. We love, and somebody turns his back and throws it in our faces, and that hurts. We hurt again and again. We want love. It's the way. So we keep at it. We love and love and love, and finally we are loved back. Then we are free from the poison of hate, bitterness, and prejudice that can destroy our lives.

Hope—there's a road for you. How can you maintain hope in a world that seems so hopeless? But somehow we believe that Christ conquers crosses. In the midst of hopelessness we still maintain that He can do it, and He did. We are free, free from despair, from discouragement, and from hopelessness.

Faith—that's the way. But it's hard to keep faith in some of the difficult circumstances that we have to endure. Yet somehow we believe that in all of our circumstances, there is Christ who loves us, who helps us, and who will not leave us. We are always in His hands. We let that kind of faith free us from anxiety, from meaninglessness, from even the fear of death itself.

That's the narrow way, to build our lives upon those values that death and time can never destroy. The way to freedom is a hard, hard way. I wonder which way have we set for our lives?

III. True freedom comes only when we make up our minds to become slaves to Christ, to give Christ thanks.

Two roads—narrow and wide, one death, one life. But the truth is that each road leads to slavery. Whenever we talk about freedom, the questions I want to ask are these: Freedom from what? Freedom to what? Human beings are made that the question is not *if* they will be free to do what they want to do, but the question is: *What* will they give their lives to? To whom? Or to what? This is our only choice—the freedom to choose to whom or what we will bow down. There has to be something that is the center of our lives. God has so made us that there is a restlessness beating inside that will never be satisfied until we take the narrow road. Since God made us, He knows what is best for us. Only when we take His Word and follow His Way will we become what He made us. That means giving up our lives to Christ. It means living our lives doing Christ's thing, living His life of love and sacrifice in all areas of our lives.

But that's not what we hear a lot. What I hear over and over again is the cry, "Do your thing as long as you don't hurt anybody but yourself." Have you heard that? Dr. Samuel Proctor, who teaches ethics at Rutgers University, pointed out two questions that ought to be asked when the cry is heard: "Do your own thing as long as you don't hurt anybody else."

How in the world do we know we never hurt anybody else? Where did we gain the wisdom to know the consequences of our total lives way down into the future. A man throws a cigarette butt into the grass, it catches fire to the grass, a forest fire comes, and the man never knew he was the cause of it. Who was the person, what was the church that turned Karl Marx off from the Christian faith? Do you know? Millions of lives have been destroyed from those whose influences caused Marx to believe that no answer was to be found in Jesus Christ. The power of influence is tremendous. Who knows what influence we will have with the angry words we speak, with the bad deeds we do, with the terrible spirits we sometimes evidence, with the acts of indifference and hate we sometimes carry out? Do what you want as long as you don't hurt anybody else, but not one of us knows if what we do will destroy a life or save it. We never know, and that's why it's safer to do Christ's thing, for we know when we do that, we're never going to destroy anybody's life.

The second question is this: *How in the world do we know that we will be able to handle the hurt we bring upon ourselves.* To do our own thing, to live life according to our laws, will one day bring something upon ourselves. Bills come due. We do reap what we sow. As Samson was the last one to know his strength was gone, how often we are the last ones to know ours is gone. Marriages have been destroyed, lives lost in alcohol, people caught in breaking the law, lives that have been miserable—all have the same common cry, "I never thought it could happen to me." But it did! The reason it did is because we live life by our own rules. We bring into our lives the tremendous power of sin. No matter how strong we think we are, we're never quite as strong as sin. If everyone can handle life as they think they can handle it, why is there so much misery, pain, emptiness, boredom, and sickness in our world today? We have discovered that when we hurt ourselves, we cannot heal ourselves. We can't do it.

Do your own thing as long as you don't hurt anybody else but yourself—that's ridiculous! That's not the way to live, it's not freedom! It is doing Christ's thing, a way that has been proven, a way that Christ showed us by His life is the only way to freedom. Live that way doing His thing, and His thing is love, sacrifice, forgiveness, hope, service, and help. "That's the way," He said. "You'll discover what it means to be free."

There's a narrow way and a wide way, and to be honest, most of us travel the wide way: it's easier, but it's deadly. You may not think so now, but one day it'll kill you. The way to freedom is only through the narrow road. The truth Christ tells us is that, if we take the way of love and sacrifice, the longer we travel down the narrow road the wider it gets, the freer we become. After all, what does it mean to be free? To be free means to be Christ's and to do Christ's thing. That's what it means to be free: to be His slave forever. Do you want to be free? There lies before you the way of the world which is wide and the way of Christ which is narrow. Your choice. I hope you choose Christ.

7
July Fourth:
Continuing the Revolution

(Luke 4:16-21)

Every year July Fourth comes to remind us that we need to celebrate the birthday of our nation. We can't miss the day. We're overwhelmed with a mass of materials that remind us of it. We hear speeches about it, read articles on it, and see many programs on TV about it. There are many events planned to celebrate it.

We know that July Fourth celebrates our nation's birthday, and we want to celebrate it because we are proud to be Americans. This is the greatest country on earth, and we are thankful to be part of it. I love America. I love America because of the high ideals it stands for, for the good that it has done, and for the hope it promises for tomorrow. To be an American is a privilege and we ought to want to celebrate it.

But we come today to worship the Lord. The worship of God reminds us that all of our thoughts and all of our lives ought to be directed to God. No matter what we serve, our highest service is rendered to God. We love America, but we ought to love God more. He is the One who is first in our lives. The Bible says "You shall have no other gods before me" (Ex. 20:3).

One god that often is before Him is the god of nationalism. But our nation is not God. To be what it ought to be, America also stands under the judgment of God. In the parable of the last judgment in Matthew 25, it's interesting to note that it is the "nations" that are judged, and we must be careful that we don't fall into the trap of equating our nation with God. We cry out for

God to bless America, but He's not going to do that unless the people in America are serious about blessing God.

So on this time when we celebrate the birthday of our nation, what can we do as Christians to celebrate it? How can we make our national birthday a good and lasting one? That is the question we need to think about. A contributor to the *Pennsylania Packet* in 1786 sounded this warning,

> The fundamental mistake of the Americans has been that they have considered the revolution as completed, when it was just begun. Having laid the pillars of the building, they ceased to exert themselves and seemed to forget the whole superstructure was then to be erected.[1]

I think they are important words to remember. We need to continue the revolution that our forefathers started long ago. Their dreams and hopes have not been realized yet, and it's up to us to help them become a reality. In fact, these basic ideas upon which our nation was founded are the same ideas that we can find in this inaugural sermon of Christ at the beginning of His ministry two thousand years ago. He went to the Temple, read from Isaiah, and talked about the love of people, about justice, and about freedom. As we think about that and about our nation, we can discover what it is we, as Christian citizens, can continue to do to help bring in, not only the kingdom of God, but a better America.

I. We must seek to continue the revolution for the worth of all persons.

One of the revolutionary ideas of our nation was that all men were created equal. Now, that isn't true in the literal sense of the word. Some of us are small, some of us are large; some are bright and some not so bright; some pretty and some not so pretty. That idea called for a respect for the dignity and worth of each individual, and it was based on the fact that all of us are created by God. We must treat persons equal in worth in the eyes of God. This is what Christ did as He walked this earth. He loved all. The poor, the oppressed, the blind, and the prisoner—all were created in the image of God and all deserve His love. At His inaugural sermon, Jesus tried to make sure the people understood that. He came to minister to all people, not just a few. All were part of His kingdom and all deserved love and respect.

This is an idea worth continuing. We need to further the respect, dignity, and love of all people. In America we have all kinds: Black and white, yellow and red, Polish and Jewish, German and Japanese, Indian and Anglo-Saxon. We have Catholic, Protestant, Jew, and agnostic, rich and poor, city boy and country girl, Northerner and Southerner, Easterner and Westerner. All of them are bound together in this country, each with their own unique characteristic and each with their own unique culture. This is what has made our country great. The Statue of Liberty has etched upon it the words of the poet Emma Lazarus:

> Give me your tired, your poor, your huddled masses yearning to breathe free, the wretched refuse of your teeming shore. Send these, the homeless, tempest-tossed to me. I lift my lamp beside the golden door.

This has been the dream of America, but we have not always lived up to that dream. Even our forefathers slipped. When they wrote the Declaration of Independence and the Constitution, there were those they did not consider worthy of equal respect. Slaves were considered only a fraction of a person in the Constitution. Women were not allowed to vote until 1920. Indians were considered savages, hardly human. Our forefathers had their prejudices, hatreds, and blind spots. We have them in our day. We still have racial violence, and prejudice and bigotry have not died. The poor are still needy and often neglected. We still despise those who don't look like we want them to look, talk like we want them to talk, or believe like we do. We have a way to go before each person gets the respect and dignity he deserves. As Christians, we ought to be demonstrating this love for all. We ought to be the ones who will reach out after all people and try to minister to them, help them, and care for them. We are the ones called by Christ to give respect and dignity to all.

Noel Mostert wrote a book entitled *Supership*. He told of a little island, Tristan da Cunha, which is located fifteen-hundred miles west of Capetown, South Africa. This island sits on the edge of the Southern Ocean. It has been called the loneliest island in the world. It is far from the main shipping lines and hammered constantly by terrifying ocean storms. Yet people there cling to each other on the island with affection. For example, back in 1964 a volcano on the island erupted and the entire population was evacuated to England, but after two years they asked to return to Tristan.

A short time later *The Cape Times* carried this story. It seems that a youngster on the island broke his leg in a hard fall. The next day a boat sailed into the harbor to take him to Capetown for medical care. As the boy lay on the stretcher at the harbor, every other man, woman, and child appeared at the top of a nearby hill; slowly, they walked down to the harbor, and each in turn went up to the boy, kissed him and wished him luck. The newspaper went on to editorialize,

> So all is well in Tristan. It is comforting to know that there is at least one spot in the world where hearts are warm and where the old ethical precepts remain. There is no racism or hatred. They want for nothing, eat well, and sleep dreamlessly, unaware that they are so laughably behind the times. The best of luck to them.[2]

When we hear a story like this, it reminds us of the goal we have here in our country. May we dedicate ourselves to do just that, to be those who foster the respect and dignity and worth of each individual.

II. We need to continue the revolution of justice for all.

"With liberty and justice for all," was an idea of our forefathers. They wanted a society in which human potential would be given a chance to be fully developed. Laws were needed to make sure that all were given their proper rights so they could live to realize their potential. Equal opportunity to be what God intended was the goal: justice and liberty for all.

Christ set out to let justice loose. In His first sermon, He said that He came to "set at liberty those who are oppressed" (Luke 4:18). He wanted to help the people wrongly mistreated. In those days, justice was not popular. The rich oppressed the poor, the Romans ruled the Jews, the courts were corrupt. Christ came to challenge all of that. He called for righteousness and fairness in the treatment of others. He called for a higher standard of living than just plain justice. He said if someone wants you to go a mile, go two. If someone wants your coat, give him your cloak also. If one hits you on the cheek, turn the other cheek to him. What He called for was justice, but also going beyond it to mercy. He wanted people to be treated fairly, to have the opportunity to realize what they could be under God.

This is what America stands for: justice and fairness to people, regardless of race, creed, and position. Everyone should be treated fairly and have an equal opportunity to live up to their potential. So the laws of the land must be fair. That's not the way it's always been, unfortunately. Sometimes to be born Black in the ghetto or Indian on a reservation does not provide the same opportunities for the enjoyment of life as it is to be born white in a mansion or in suburbia. To be poor and convicted of a crime is deadly because the poor cannot afford comparable legal advice as the rich. Justice often comes to those who can pay for it, and if one can't, that's too bad. Our prisons are far too full of the poor and the needy.

The cost of education past high school is high and many who deserve it are not able to get it. Our tax system has loopholes that usually favor the rich and make the poor poorer. There is still too much discrimination in jobs against women and minority groups. The test of the nation is what it does for the least of its people.

Does it strive to improve their quality of life, does it seek to protect and encourage them? The greatness of a nation is that it seeks justice for all people, especially the least of them.

In March 1970, CBS television conducted a national random telephone survey regarding public opinion on the Bill of Rights. The results were alarming. Seventy-six percent of the 1136 people interviewed believed extremist groups should not be permitted to organize demonstrations against the government, even if there appeared to be no danger of violence. Fifty-four percent would not give everyone the right to criticize the government if the criticism were thought to be damaging to the national interest. Fifty-five percent felt the newspapers, radio, and television should not be allowed to report stories which the government considered harmful to national interest.

The Christian Life Commission of the Southern Baptist Convention, in cooperation with the Research Services Department of the Baptist Sunday School Board, took a sample support of personal freedoms among leaders of the Southern Baptist Convention, using the CBS survey. Results of this poll were equally outstanding. Consider this: sixty-seven percent of the respondents would be willing to restrict peaceful assembly. Fifty-nine percent would be willing to restrict the right to a free press. Fifty-two percent would be willing to restrict the right concerning freedom of religion.[3]

We have a long way to go before we have liberty and justice for all. As Christians, we are to be the ones to try to bring it to be. We are to be the ones "to preach good news to the poor./ . . . to proclaim release to the captives and . . ./ to set at liberty those who are oppressed" (Luke 4:18). Someone was asked once why he opposed slavery? He said simply, "Because it is wrong." As Christians, we ought to oppose injustice wherever we see it because it is wrong. We are to work to make this a better country for all people. That revolution needs to be continued.

III. We need to continue the revolution for freedom with responsibility.

We are called the "land of the free." We are to be free from tyrants, from kings who would use people for their own ends. Our forefathers set out to provide an atmosphere where we could have a part in governing ourselves, so we have a representative government where, through elected representatives, we can express our opinions. We have a participatory government where we can take part in shaping and determining our policies. We have a democratic government where each person's vote and life are important.

So we have freedom, not just *from* tyranny but *for* democracy. The story goes that when our government was founded on July 4, 1776, someone asked Dr. Benjamin Franklin, "What do we have, a republic or a monarchy?" Franklin replied, "A republic, if you can keep it." Responsible freedom, this is what we are seeking, to give people the freedom to do what they want to, be what they want, as long as they don't harm others and destroy our world.

But it's hard work to keep it. Christ tried to say that, too. He proclaimed freedom and liberty. In His inaugural sermon He came to proclaim "release to the captives . . . to set at liberty those who are oppressed." They were to be free, not to do what they wanted but to do what Christ wanted. They were to be free to be slaves to Christ. They were to use their freedom in responsible ways. Such freedom is not easily kept. In Maxwell Anderson's play, *Valley Forge,* Washington joined a group of his bedraggled and dispirited soldiers in the shelter of an old barn. In a moving speech, he burned into their consciousness the true nature of their plight. "I promise those who follow me further, no chance of victory, for, by my God, I see none; no glory or gain, or laurels returning home, but wounds and death—cold, disease, and hunger, winter to come such as this you have, with our blood trail in the snow and no end to it till you shovel each other in with those at Valley Forge." And later, when they had finished their heart-breaking task of burying their dead comrades, Washington turned to his men and said,

"This liberty will look easy by and by when nobody dies to get it."[4]

How true that sounds. Few of us face death daily to keep our freedom, but the countless crosses in our cemeteries ought to remind us that freedom does not come cheaply, nor is freedom maintained cheaply. We have to continue to work at it. The comedian, Will Rogers, once said, "The history of American can be written in three phrases: the passing of the Indian, the passing of the buffalo, and the passing of the buck."[5] It cannot be. We, who are citizens of this country, must not pass the buck to someone else. If we do not like the way things are, we must quit sitting around blaming others. Instead, we must set out trying to make them the way they ought to be. We are gifted with freedom, but freedom must be held responsibly.

So, Ben Franklin, what do we have, "a republic or a monarchy?" A republic, if you can keep it." I hope we want to keep it. It was a noble experiment our fathers started, but the revolution they began is not over, and it will never be. We are pilgrims in search of a dream, but a great dream, a dream that we must never let die. For it's the dream that Christ has given. It's a dream that He wants us to live daily: where we have respect for the dignity and worth of each individual, where we have a desire for justice and righteousness for all, where we want people to have freedom to live life responsibly. It's a worthy dream.

Do we feel it's worthy enough to keep alive? There was that moment when our forefathers had to make the decision. Would they sign the Declaration of Independence? To sign it meant they could lose their property and their lives. To sign it was a tremendous risk; never again would they be the same. They had to make a choice. Was their signing worth their lives? They took the pen, signed their names, and began a revolution that is not yet over. Now they look at us. In a sense, the Declaration of Independence is there for us to sign, too. Will we feel that the ideals of America are worth our signature, worth our commitment? Will we believe

that the ideals—really the ideals that Christ cried for—are worth
our lives? The revolution is looking for more recruits. We are
asked to sign. Will we put our names down?

Notes

1. C. Welton Gaddy, *Proclaim Liberty* (Nashville: Broadman Press, 1975), 116.

2. Ernest T. Campbell, "Let the State Be the State," Sermons from Riverside,
Riverside Church of New York City, 6 July 1975, 9-10.

3. C. Welton Gaddy, *Profile of a Christian Citizen* (Nashville: Broadman Press, 1974),
38.

4. Alvin C. Porteous, "Reflections of a New Citizen," *The Pulpit,* XIVII, no. 7, July
1956, 13.

5. Leighton Ford, "Spiritual Values: The Number One National Priority," Pro-
ceedings of The Christian Life Commission Seminar, Southern Baptist Convention,
"National Priorities and Christian Responsibility," New York City, 1-3 March
1971, 7.

8

Labor Day:
Putting Work into Life Under God

(2 Tim. 2:15)

He was an active member of the church. In fact, he taught Sunday School and served on the Finance Committee. He also owned a department store and paid some of the lowest wages in town. The working conditions at his department store were far from ideal. It was even known that some of the business deals he made were quite shady. There was a gap between what he professed to believe and the way he ran his department store. One day someone mentioned that to him. He said simply, "What I believe has nothing to do with the way I run my business. Church is church, and business is business. Religion should keep it's nose out of people's work. It has no business being there."

Is that right? Should faith be divorced from all the areas of our life, like work or play or school? Does faith deal only with spiritual matters and with spiritual things, heaven and not earth? Does it matter what we do with our lives if we are Christians?

There are those who say that Christianity only deals with the spiritual side of life, but I can't believe that the Bible supports that. The Bible is a book about people involved in life and work. Jesus Himself was a carpenter who knew what it was to have blisters on His hands from hard work. Many of the disciples were fishermen. Paul earned his living by making tents. Paul was the one who told the Christians at Thessalonica who had quit work to wait for the second coming, "Go back to work." He uttered the famous words, "If any one will not work, let him not eat" (2 Thess. 3:10).

The Bible is not on the side of divorcing faith from life. It's not on the side of laziness, either. The Bible deals with a Christ who came to be the Redeemer of all of life, not part of it. Jesus is Lord of all life: our work, our play, our home, or anything else we do with it. If what we believe does not spill over in the way we live our lives, then we have vastly misunderstood faith.

Our faith ought to make a difference in our work. *Work* has become a very agonizing word in our day. With automation and mass production, our work is often boring and tedious. By the way, no matter what profession you enter, you will find some parts of it boring and tedious. A touchdown pass is caught, but it comes after hours and hours of practice on the field. An actor plays a part, but there are hours and hours of rehearsal that were not always exciting. A book is written after hours of agonizing labor and pain to produce it. Every work has parts that are boring and tedious. How can we make it better? How can we bring work alive to us? How can we put work back into life and life back into our work? For the many who just go to work to get by and live, how can it become more exciting?

As Christians, work ought to be something special. We should to be able to look upon work with a different perspective. We see work as a calling, an opportunity to reveal what we think about God and life. Work reveals our values and faith. What we do with our lives reveals what we believe.

Paul wrote to Timothy, a young man entering the ministry, about his work. He gave some good advice to Timothy. If he remembered what Paul said, Timothy's work would be alive, not boring and routine. Let us see what Paul told Timothy and realize what we can do to reveal our faith in our work.

I. What we do reveals what we believe.

Timothy went into a profession that would be pleasing to God. He was going into the ministry to "rightly" divide "the word of truth" (KJV). He was going to preach. Timothy would not be ashamed of that. He would be doing something honorable. What Timothy did would be a testimony to everybody that here was someone whose beliefs were deep and rich. He did what was pleasing to God.

Everything we do ought to be pleasing to God. Our career ought to be honorable. Is it? A publisher of a crude, pornographic magazine was "converted" and became part of the born-again Christian movement. After the publisher's conversion, there was one thing he did not do. He did not give up publishing the magazine. Since he did not, his witness is quite stained. He lost a great deal of credibility. People wondered, *How could somebody who professes faith in Christ as Savior and Lord be involved in that kind of work?*

There are a lot of honorable professions in our world. Our work ought to be something we feel called into. It should be what God wants you to do and where God wants you to be. Is that the way you have gone about your career? There will be struggles because many of the careers are difficult. Each person has to decide what is right for him or for her. Whatever we do, we ought to make sure we do it without any fear of it being dishonorable, displeasing God. If God came and stood next to us at our workplace, would we be ashamed?

John Jefferson told about Wilkes Booth, the actor, who ran the theatre behind the scenes as if it were a church. There were some Christians in those days who thought that going to the theatre was sinful. One clergyman called Booth and said, "Is there some back door through which we can slip? Several of us want to come to see the play. Is there some back door that we can come through, and nobody can see us?" Booth said, "No! There is no door in this theatre through which God cannot see."[1]

This is how we ought to be living and working, with the confidence that there is nothing we do that we would be ashamed of God seeing. What we do ought to reveal to others what we believe about the high values of life.

II. Why we do our work can reveal our faith.

"Do your best to present yourself to God as . . . a workman who has no need to be ashamed." Timothy did what was honorable, but why did he do it? Timothy did it because of his response to the grace of God in his life. He did it because he saw in it an opportunity to serve God, to bring others into the joy of the Kingdom that he knew. To serve God, to serve others—that was the reason Timothy did what he did.

Timothy's motives were good motives and they ought to be ours. What is the meaning of the work you do? Why do you do it? I read of a man who was given a gold watch after several years of service on the railroad. All he did during these years of service was that before every train left the station, the man would take a hammer and hit every wheel of the train. Somebody said, "Why did you do that?" He said, "I really don't know. They told me to hit the hammer on the wheel and for twenty-five years that's what I've been doing." He apparently never knew he was supposed to be listening for a special sound that revealed whether the wheel was cracked or not.[2]

I hope we don't do our work with such lack of purpose. Why are we doing what we're doing? Just to make money? Just to survive? If that's the reason, then our work will be dull, tedious, and agonizing. We ought to see our work as an opportunity to serve God and others. Our work ought to be an offering to God. What we do should make this world a better place. If our work is not trying to help others to become better than they are, if our work is not contributing to the development of this life in which we live, then we need to reexamine what we do and why we do it.

There was a man in England who was very active in church: a Sunday School teacher, lay leader, and served on its boards and agencies. He was a baker by trade. One day he was traveling on a train, and an overzealous lady came over and said, "Are you a Christian?' He said, "Yes, I am." Then she said, "What are you doing to serve God?" He said, "I bake bread." "I didn't ask you what you did for a living, I said what are you doing to serve the Redeemer?" He said, "I bake bread." She continued on, irritated by it all. "I didn't ask that. I said what are you doing to bring honor and glory to God?" He said, "I bake bread."[3]

Is this what we say about our work? "I clean the house; I fix or make cars; I serve on ships; I sell merchandise; I cook food; I teach; I do what I do, and it is offered as service to God."

III. The way we do our work reveals what we believe.

"Do your best . . . rightly handling the word of truth." That's what Timothy was told. "Do your best"! Timothy would make mistakes. He would not be a perfect preacher. He would preach sometimes, and nobody would listen. He would say and do the wrong thing and probably make some people mad. That would be all right because they would be mistakes of honesty, mistakes made because Timothy was an imperfect human being. Timothy was not asked to be perfect. He was asked to do his best.

If there's anyone who ought to be giving an honest day's work for an honest day's pay, it ought to be those of us who bear the name *Christian.* We ought to work hard. We ought to do the best that we can. We ought never try to attempt less than our best. Christans ought to do their best.

Let me introduce you to two men. One is a Japanese man who runs a furniture shop that's famous for its inlaid furniture and work on furniture tabletops. A tourist was in the shop wanting to buy a particular tabletop. The man wouldn't sell it. The tourist offered all sorts of money, but the owner still wouldn't sell it. He said, "I won't sell it because there is a flaw on that tabletop." The tourist said, "I can't see it, and nobody else that I know will be able to notice if there's a flaw in that tabletop." The Japanese man said, "I know it, and I will never let anything go out of my shop that is imperfect." I wish we had a lot more people like that.[4]

Here is another man who worked in a weaving factory. Mr.

Adkins was his name. His pastor was going through the mill one day. The pastor said to the foreman, "I suppose Mr. Adkins is one of your best weavers." The foreman said, "No, he isn't, unfortunately. Mr. Adkins spends time talking about religion when he ought to be sitting at his loom. He has great capacity to be a fine weaver, but the problem with Mr. Adkins is that he doesn't understand that when he is here at the factory, his religion ought to come through his fingers, not from his mouth."[5]

The places where we work: Does our religion come through our fingers, hands, feet, and minds? We ought to be doing the best job we can at the tasks we have. That is a tremendous Christian witness that we can give in the places where we work. To do the best we can, that's all God asks.

Too many of us have divorced faith from life. What we believe in church on Sunday, we don't live on Monday. That may be the reason our lives are not as full as we want them to be, that we struggle through life with discouragement and disappointment, not with joy and confidence. We have kept God boxed up in a building and not let Him into the world where we live. Our work ought to be under God. We must realize that *what* we do, *why* we do it, and the *way* we do it are our testimony to whether or not we believe God is indeed Lord of all life.

A young man was choosing a profession and went to see an old, canal-boat captain, a friend of the family. He asked, "What should I do?" The canal-boat captain said, "What are you good at?" He said, "Soaps and candles." The captain said, "O.K. Do the best you can with soaps and candles and take God into partnership with you. Remember to give him a tenth of all you make and remember that you need God in all of it." The young man took the captain's advice. His name was William Colgate, a very successful businessman. He was the first president of the American Bible Society; Colgate University was named after him. Colgate was a man who went into his work in partnership with God, giving Him the honor and glory for what he did, serving Him through what he did.[6]

If we will do our work in partnership with God and stay with it, our work will come alive to us and others. Many will realize that what we do, we do because of what we believe about God.

Notes

1. Harry Emerson Fosdick, "The Sacred and the Secular Are Inseparable," *The Twentieth Century Pulpit*, ed. James W. Cox (Nashville: Abingdon, 1978), 62-63.

2. John Bishop, "God in a Workman's Jacket," *The Clergy Journal* (August, 1977): 13.

3. Larry D. Wilkinson, "A Gospel of Labor," *Pulpit Digest* (September/October, 1979): 6.

4. William Barclay, *In the Hands of God* (New York: Harper & Row, 1966), 57-58.

5. C. Thomas Hilton, "The Best Dressed Woman in Town," *The Clergy Journal* (April 1979): 9.

6. *Pulpit Resource* (January-March, 1978): 18.

Part II:
Special Church Days

9
Parent/Child Dedication:
Hannah—Dedicating a Child and a Home

(1 Sam. 1:19-28)

A parent-child dedication service can be a meaningful experience. Only time will tell how meaningful it is. For we all know that words spoken in commitment must be lived out with deeds done. It is easier to say the words than to live them. For our homes to be Christian, it will take hard and dedicated work.

It is important that we give it, for the home is the greatest theological seminary in the world. Our children will learn more about God from the home and in the home than any other place. We don't really have to say much to teach children about God. Our attitudes at home, the deeds we do there, and the values we live by there, are all teaching our children how important God is or isn't. What we live for and the way we live defines their understanding of God. It is very important that we commit ourselves to making our homes Christian.

What is involved in that? That's why I want to talk about Hannah, the mother of Samuel, who came and dedicated her child to God. In doing so, she pointed out three important principles to know as we try to keep our homes Christian.

I. We must never forget who gives us our children.

Hannah had been the laughingstock of the community for a long time because she wanted to have children, but didn't. In those days, childlessness was a bad thing. So Hannah prayed earnestly to God for a child, and Samuel was born. She went to God's house and praised God. She thanked Him for His goodness and, in doing that, showed that she remembered where Samuel came from. He was God's precious gift to her. She was thankful for him and for all the days of her life Hannah would not forget that God gave her the blessing of a child.

We say that's common sense, we know that. Children are the gift of God. By the way, parents are, too. All of us are created in the image of God. That's common sense, but it is worth remembering. It ought to tell us a couple of things.

For one thing, we ought to act like the children of God at home. A boy was going off to college and expected that lecture from his parents about how he should behave. All during the preparations of getting ready to go, the boy was waiting any moment for his parents to sit him down and tell him what he could do and what he couldn't do in college. But he never got such a lecture. Instead, as he boarded the bus to leave, his father told him one thing, "Son, in whatever you do, remember whose son you are." To remember whose son he was, would help him live up to those standards.

In the home, do we remember whose children we are? We are the children of God, but do we act like it in the way we try to live in the home? I will never forget that college student from Tennessee who told me, "Back home my parents are the pillars of the church, but they are hell to live with." How is it in our homes? Do we put on a good show at church, but home is a different matter? Do we as parents, young people, and children strive to act like children of God? Are we kind, patient, and sympathetic? Do we love one another? One of the needs in the home is for us to remember whose we are. We are God's, and we need to act like it.

But the other application of that is this: We need to *treat* each other as children of God. One of the tragedies of our time is child abuse: parents who beat and neglect their children. We wonder how this could happen. Sometimes we fall into the mistake of believing that children are our possessions. Children are not possessions; they are persons created in the image of God. They are His, and they are to be treated with respect, dignity, and courtesy. Do we try to be sympathetic? Do we try to understand? Do we listen? Do we provide for their needs? Do we try to love them? Do children try to treat parents the same way? To understand them, to be sensitive to their needs? It's a mutual way of living in the home—to try to treat one another with the respect and dignity due a child of God because that's who everyone is.

Some years ago a man of small physical stature entered a motel. The motel operator was so unimpressed by the man's appearance that she told him she could not provide a room for that night. Her daughter came into the office at that moment, looked at the man, and recognized him. She quickly called her mother aside and whispered that the man she had turned away was a distinguished musician, conductor of a symphony orchestra. The motel operator called him back and offered all kinds of apologies. She said, "Why, of course we can take care of you. Why didn't you tell me you were somebody?" As the man turned angrily away from the desk and headed back to his car, he said to her, "Madame, everybody is somebody."[1]

Sometimes in the home, we forget that each one is a person created in the image of God and of great value. We are to treat each other with that kind of awareness and sensitivity.

II. We must seek to be good stewards of our children's lives, to train them well.

This is what Hannah did when she came to dedicate Samuel to the Lord. She realized that motherhood was a great privilege, but it was also a tremendous responsibility. It mattered to God what she did with Samuel. It was important for her to train Samuel in such a way that he would know who his God was.

That is an important aspect of parenting. God lends us our children and expects us to be good teachers and trainers of them, to prepare them for that time when He will want them back. It's like putting my money in a bank. I trust that banker to take good care of my money, to be a good steward of it, to use it well. If he loses it, misplaces it, or steals it, then I won't like that; I'll try to have him put in jail. I certainly will take my money out of that bank. In a sense, God gives us children, and He expects us to be a good steward of their lives. He expects us to train them to be His children. Is that what we are doing in our homes?

Do we teach our children to pray? Do we pray with them? Do we read our Bibles with our children and help them to understand it? Do we teach our children to love all people regardless of color of skin or where they were born? Do we teach our children to be kind to one another, to be sensitive to the needs of others? Are we teaching our children that it matters what is right and what is wrong, that to live honestly is the best way to live? Are we teaching our children to support the church and worship by our support of it ourselves?

Some statistics came out that surprised me. When a mother and father both go to church and bring their children with them, 72 percent of the children grow up and stay in the church. When just the father comes, 55 percent stay with the church. When just the mother comes—and this is the shocking statistic—only 15 percent stay with the church. If neither parent comes, only 6 percent of the children stay with the church.[2] When the parents will not support church worship, it sends a message to the children that, when they grow up, they won't have to take church and worship seriously.

What kind of example are we leaving our children? What kind of training are we giving them? It is important what kind of stewards we are of their lives. At a school for juvenile delinquents in Iowa, they took some boys and girls and asked them, "If you could be a parent, what would you do with your children to keep from happening to your children what is happening to you?" They worked out a program, and it had four basic principles in it. The first thing they wanted was religious training, the second was a good education, the third was companionship in the home, and the fourth, discipline.[3] Did you get that? What these children said they needed in the home was religious training, good education, companionship, and discipline. We worry a lot about prayer in the schools, maybe we ought to worry a little bit more about prayer in the homes. I like the little boy who came up to his daddy and said, "Daddy, let's play a game of darts. I'll throw the dart, and you just say, 'Wonderful.' "[4]

You know it might not be a bad idea to give our children that kind of love and support, to help them understand through our love, the love of God.

III. We need to give our children away to God.

That was what Hannah did. She left Samuel in the care of Eli, because she wanted Samuel to grow up to serve God. How she loved Samuel to do that for him! She wanted Samuel to know God and wanted God to have Samuel, and she gave him away. "As long as he lives," she said, "he is lent to the Lord" (v. 28). Samuel did grow up to be a great prophet and leader of Israel, and I think you can trace it back to these moments when Hannah said to God, "Here is Samuel, he is all yours."

This is what we are here to do as parents. God gives us our children, but only for a while. A day will come when He will ask for them back. Are we preparing them for that moment when God will want them in His service? Are we trying to develop our children to try to follow the will of God or our wills? Are we trying to teach them that joy in life is doing what He wants? Every now and then someone asks me, "Do you want any of your children to become a preacher?" My first response to that is, "No way." But yet the truth is that I would be proud if one of my children became a minister.

But my children must not become ministers to please me. They should not become *anything* to please me. What they have to do is to become what God calls them to do and be. I don't know what that is. I can't decide for them and we can't decide for our children either. Too often we want children to do what we have done, but children must grow up and do what God wants them to do. Are we training them to do that? That's the important matter.

It's risky because God may ask our children to do some difficult things. He may call some of them to be ministers or missionaries in some far place or to be involved in the struggle for liberty and justice for all. As parents, it is tough to watch our children accept such responsibilities and do such deeds. I remember a couple in Texas whose daughter married a missionary, and they were commissioned to serve in South America. The father told me, "The hardest moment of my life was when I had to watch them leave to go there, knowing that I would not see them for several years. But it was also the most joyous day in my life because I knew that she was going to serve God and that we had done our job as parents well. We had helped her understand that life is found in serving Him." The best thing we can ever do for our children is to help prepare them to hear the call of God and follow Him.

We need to dedicate our homes to Christ. We need, like Hannah, to dedicate our children to God. Samuel became a great prophet and leader of God. Someone has said, "Maybe the reason we don't have more Samuels today is because we don't have more Hannahs." That may be true. What I hope we will do is never forget who gave us to each other. All of us are the gift of God. I hope that we will treat each other as such. May we try to train our children in the way they should go, the way of God. What we should desire to do more than anything else for our children is to give them to God, to let Him use them however He wants.

I think the best way to do that is to try to surround them with the love that we have discovered from God. There's a little vignette by Ernest Lawson, entitled, "You Try Love, and I'll Try Ajax." It's a little letter written by a boy to his mother and it says:

Dear Mom:
    I have decided that you, and not I, are the casualty in the battle of the bedroom. Yes, my bedroom is a mess. Yes, it's true you don't ask me to do much, but will wars end because I make my bed? Will

all hunger in the world end because I hang up my clothes? Will all the terrible things happening in the world today, with them all, what does the condition of one bedroom matter? Yes, I know that before the world can be put in order, each person must put his own little world in order. But dust doesn't bother my world. To put my world in order, I need love, not Ajax. So Mom, I'll make you a deal. You use a little more love, and I'll use a little more Ajax."[5]

As I read that, I thought that may be right. Sometimes we do get our priorities mixed up in the home. The greatest priority is to make sure that our homes are full of the love that we have discovered in Christ. I hope that we will dedicate ourselves to living that love.

Notes

1. David MacLennan, *Sermons of Faith and Hope* (Valley Forge, PA: Judson Press, 1971), 66.

2. David H. C. Read, "Making Families Holy," Sermon from Madison Avenue Presbyterian Church, New York City, 28 December 1980, 4.

3. *Pulpit Resource* (October, November, December, 1982): 31.

4. *Pulpit Resource* (April, May, June, 1984): 20.

5. *Pulpit Resource* (October, November, December, 1980): 36.

10
Pentecost Sunday:
When Pentecost Comes, What Happens to Us?

(Acts 2:1-4,43-47)

The preacher begins to preach and it's like you've heard so many times before. He talks about the world and what bad shape it's in. He says it's in bad shape because of what we are. We are not the people we need to be, we need to change our ideas, attitudes, and the way we live. If we do that, then maybe the world could become a better place. Then the preacher puts in the kicker. He says, "What we need is for Pentecost to happen again. We need another Pentecost."

What was he talking about? What did he mean by Pentecost? We know that Pentecost was a Jewish festival held fifty days after the sabbath that followed Passover. It was a regular expected occasion and celebrated yearly. But when the preacher was talking about Pentecost, surely he meant more than just a celebration of a Jewish festival. Instead, he was referring to something different that happened in one particular celebration of Pentecost: something unforgettable.

Remember the background. Christ had gone away from the disciples, and they were waiting for the Spirit to come. When the Spirit came, they were overwhelmed by a sense of the presence and the power of Christ. The events that followed brought a harmony of spirits. The preaching of the gospel followed, and 3,000 were saved. It was a tremendous experience, and we do need it again. But what does it mean *when Pentecost comes?* What exactly will happen to us?

I. When Pentecost comes, we will worship expectantly.

One of the experiences they had was true worship of God. It was an ecstatic praise and thanksgiving. There was talk about speaking in tongues. They praised God in unknown languages. The language they knew was not quite adequate; they needed more. It was a praise offered to God, a joyful experience. But we need to notice a condition of this worship. In verse I, "they were all together in one place." They had been told to wait; and they were waiting, expecting the promise of Christ to be fulfilled. If they had not been there expecting a blessing, chances are they would not have gotten it.

Here is a point we need to think seriously about. What is the purpose of worship? Often we have some serious misunderstandings about worship. You can hear it in some of the statements people make. Some ask "Did you like church today?" which implies that worship is entertainment. You go to "like" the song or "like" the sermon. If you don't "like" it, then it's been a waste of time. But worship is not a service where you come to be entertained. The question is not whether you liked it, but whether or not a true word of God came to you, challenged you, and changed you.

Then you hear some people make the comment, "I didn't get anything out of church today." Well, what did they want? A particular kind of feeling, pleasure, or sense of guilt? What is it that they were expecting to get? The question is not What did you get out of it? but What did you give to it?

We call this moment on Sunday a worship *service.* It is an offering of ourselves to God. In that offering, hopefully, God will reaffirm Himself in our lives. We must come to give in order to receive, we must come expecting in order to find.

The disciples were waiting; they were ready. When we come Sunday after Sunday, are we ready for the blessings and the promises of God? The presence of God comes when we worship and praise God for what He has done and has given.

During the Korean War, a story came out of North Korea about a group of Americans held prisoners by the Communists. But they found a way to conduct worship services under the very noses of their captors. Such activity was forbidden. Even so, these Christians managed to gather in a circle in the prison yard and give the appearance of being engaged in an in consequential bull session. Once assembled they murmured softly so the guards couldn't understand, "Holy, holy, holy! Lord God Almighty! Early in the morning our song shall rise to thee." These prisoners were ailing, semistarved; they knew that they were at the mercy of the guards; their clothes were ragged; their faces thin and bearded. All in all, they were as unlikely a congregation of worshipers as anyone could imagine. Watching them were armed Communists, better dressed, better fed, very much the conquerors. The prison yard was filled with mud and snow. Stained glass, organ music, and safety were miles away. But it was a place of worship because the prisoners praised God for what He meant to them.[1] It was a place of worship because they expected, yes needed, the presence of God among them. There in that prison was a Pentecost. May it happen to us where we gather expectantly to worship the Lord.

II. When Pentecost comes, we will witness unashamedly.

Their worship was exciting, and passers by thought they were drunk, but Peter said that it wasn't so. Here was Peter, that uneducated fisherman who often said and did the wrong things at the wrong times! Peter, who had denied Christ in the darkness! But this same Peter stood and began to talk about what it meant to follow Christ. Then they began to share Christ with each other unashamedly. They were no longer hiding their commitment to Christ. They were ready to tell. As a result of their witness, 3,000 people were saved and, as the days went by, more were brought into the Kingdom. They no longer hid their light under a bushel.

We all know a Christian ought to be a witness. In fact, we know Christians *are* witnesses; we can't help it. We will be good ones or bad ones by the way we live. But when it comes to sharing our witness verbally, most of us have more difficulty. We are shy or afraid to do it. We don't know how to do it or what to say. We are afraid we won't have all the answers people want. Notice what happened before the people at Pentecost witnessed. They experienced the presence of Christ. Then, they shared what they had experienced.

One of our problems has been with the way we teach other people how to witness. We teach people the plan of salvation, or Roman road of salvation, and people learn that and go out to tell it. Unfortunately, sometimes we become more interested in sharing the plan than our own personal experience of Christ. Witness is basically sharing what we know about Christ, what has happened in our lives because of Christ. What difference has happened to us since Christ has come? How has He helped us? What has He meant to us? Do we have anything to say about that? This is what we have to share. We don't have to memorize that testimony, we just have to tell it. Maybe the reason we don't want to visit or witness is because we don't have much of anything to share.

Has Christ come to us? If He has, we have something to say. To learn all the other Scriptures and ideas that can help people toward the faith is good, but primarily what we need to be doing is unashamedly saying, "This is what Christ has done for me." We need to be witnesses for Christ in this world.

One of the great black gospel singers was Mahalia Jackson. Fame never went to her head. She always remained the humble, devout Christian servant. A close friend was telling about the time Mahalia sang on a television show. Her friend said she was singing "A City Called Heaven," and as she got into it she closed her eyes and the tears streamed down her cheeks. Before she knew it she cried out, "O glory," on the air. Then she remembered where she was and said, "Pardon me, CBS, I forgot where I was." The calls came in from everywhere. She couldn't contain it as she was singing and remembering all that Christ meant and all that Christ would do.[2] It had to come out! When Pentecost happens, our joy will come out, too. We need to witness; that's a sign that Pentecost has come.

III. When Pentecost comes, we will care for each other and our needs.

They began to share not only their faith but their possessions with each other. They shared all they had. Here's the point to remember. They cared for one another, they sought to meet each other's needs. When the Spirit got hold of them, He found specific expression in caring for one's neighbor. They were putting the gospel into practice. They put their lives to work ministering to both the physical and spiritual needs of one another.

One of my concerns is that many folks who talk about having a Pentecost are thinking in terms of a spiritual revival only, to save souls and change hearts, get people right with God and each other. That's necessary. But we must not neglect this other part of Pentecost. We must not forget that Pentecost results in ministering to the physical needs of people. Someone says, "Our job is to get people into heaven." I also think we have a responsibility to bring heaven into earth. We are to strive to build up the Kingdom on earth as it is in heaven, as Jesus' Model Prayer reminds us. I think the teaching is clear. We need the deep devotional and spiritual side of the faith. We need to pray, meditate, confess, worship, and sit at the feet of Jesus. But it is no good if we never let what we have experienced inside get outside. We must enflesh our love, joy, and hope. Our physical experiences must result in physical actions. Not to do this is to miss what Pentecost is about.

How do we know if we had a Pentecost? Do we desire to meet the needs of each other? Pentecost leads us to do both, to battle the spiritual problems of pride, prejudice, unbelief, indifference, and sin. But Pentecost also leads us to deal with poverty, ignorance, illiteracy, sickness, injustice, and hunger. We can't attack one problem without attacking the others. We can't love God without expressing it in specific ways of love. And we can't just meet the needs of people without the spiritual motivation inside. Pentecost calls for both.

A missionary was giving an address to some Hindu ladies. One of them got up and walked out. After a short absence she returned and listened more intently than before. At the close, the missionary asked if she had left because she was not interested. The Hindu replied,

> O yes, I was so interested in the wonderful things you were saying that I went out to ask your carriage driver whether you meant it and whether you lived it at home. He said that you did so I came back to listen again.[3]

We are being watched to see if we believe what we say we do. We talk about love: we are watched to see if we will do it. We talk about hope: we are watched to see if we will do it. We talk about mercy, but we are watched to see if we practice it. We talk about justice, and we are watched to see if we do it. If Pentecost comes, not only do we talk about what we believe, we *do* what we believe.

I would agree with the preacher who said we need another Pentecost experience. We need such experiences over and over again. We need to notice this: Pentecost happened, but it did not last long. The early Christians began to form churches but in those churches they began to fight and argue with one another. They began to commit immorality. They began to divide into groups and to be suspicious of one another. They fell into spiritual pride. Pentecost happened, but it was easily forgotten in the passing of time. That's why we need Pentecost again. That's why we try to have one every Sunday. We need to once again worship God, praising Him for all He's done. We need to once again share the spiritual blessings He's given us, committing ourselves to share the material blessings with those who need it!

Pentecost can come! The presence and power of God is available for us now, but we must want it. We must expect it. Every moment when we come together to worship, every moment when we come together to pray and to sing His praises, every moment when we come together in the name of the Lord, it's an opportunity for Pentecost to happen. May God bring it again!

Notes

1. John Townsend, "Worship: Option or Opportunity?" *Pulpit Preaching* (June 1970): 13.

2. Gerald Kennedy, "I Forgot Where I Was," *Pulpit Digest* (November 1956): 76.

3. Ira C. Starling, Jr., "The Sermon That You Preach," *The New Pulpit Digest* (May-June 1973): 49.

11

Ascension Sunday:
What Does the Ascension Have to Do with Me?

(Heb. 7:25)

A boy was asked by his father what he had learned in Sunday School. The boy said, "They told about the exciting battle of Jericho." He told more about it. He said, "Joshua and his forces were having trouble, so he had to call in some tanks and some artillery support. He had some planes to come and drop their bombs into the city and the right flank attacked from one side, the left flank from the other side, and after a fierce battle, with lots of hand-to-hand combat, Jericho fell." The father looked amazed and said, "Did they really teach you that?" The boy said, "No, but I had to make it more interesting because if you heard it like I did, it would be dull."

For many, the Bible is a dull book. They feel it's an outdated book with outdated words. People have a hard time trying to understand what the Bible has to say, what it's about. Even among those of us who feel the Bible is so important, we often disagree on how to interpret it. We've often ranted and raved at each other about what the Bible means, so we've lost the truth that the Bible may be trying to convey. There's a story of a prince who fell in love with a poor girl who was very beautiful. The prince, being a very wealthy person, was accustomed to the best. He had polish, refinement, and was quite sophisticated. The poor girl, on the other hand, had none of these advantages. Her life was plain and drab by comparison. The prince became infatuated with the girl and sent her a beautiful sapphire. He wrapped it in exquisite paper and tied a magnificent ribbon around it. As the story goes, the poor girl, because of her poverty, had never seen anything as lovely as the wrappings, and in her excitement and joy, she never got past them and the real treasure that she was meant to have.[1]

We must not miss the real treasures that the Bible has for us. For instance, take the account of the ascension. It seems so strange and distant to us. Christ left the disciples and disappeared into the heavens above. What does that have to do with us in our world, with our problems and our hurts and our cares? What does such a strange story have to do with us? It's a very important and vital word for each of us today because it is a word about life and how we can live it. The writer of Hebrews talked about the meaning of the ascension in the verses of our Scripture and it tells us what the ascension has to do with us.

I. The ascension reemphasizes the truth that God is a God who is for us, not against us.

The author used the phrase "exalted above the heavens" (v. 26). This was a reference to the ascension. Christ had gone to sit at the right hand of God. Heaven, of course, was the place where God dwelled. Now Christ had gone to dwell there. Here is the picture. At Bethlehem, Christ had come to reveal God, to let mankind know that God loved and cared for all of them. In the garden of Eden, there was a great mistrust of God. Adam and Eve thought God was trying to work against them, but Christ came to identify with us, to live where we live, to suffer what we suffer, all for the purpose of reuniting us with God, to tell us that God is for us, not against us. This Christ, that they had lived with and had come to love, was going to sit on the right hand of God. He was their friend, now not only on earth, but also in heaven.

God is for us. He is our friend in heaven, rooting for us to keep the faith. Here is a most important word to us. Often we begin to wonder if God isn't trying to work against us, to keep us from enjoying life. Do we ever get mistrustful of God? We go through some suffering and tragedy, we don't understand it, and we ask God, "Why? Why did You do this to us?" It seems as if He's against us. We feel guilty, and we feel that God is trying to punish us because of what has happened. We can't sleep at night because of the guilt, and it seems as if God is against us. We look at the burdens and problems that so often seem too much for us to handle, and we feel that God doesn't really care about us, or He wouldn't let us have to struggle so much. It seems that God is against us. We look at what God requires and demands of us. We're to die to live. We're to take up a cross. It sounds as if He wants to take life away, not give it. God asks too much of us it seems. It seems that He might indeed be against us.

But the ascension reminds us that it is not so. Christ came, lived with us, and died for us. He came to save us from our own destruction. He did not come to destroy us. Without Christ we would have little hope for anything in life. We would have no answer for our difficulties, no hope. Even now, God is working through the Spirit of Christ to help us. In the midst of suffering and tragedy, we may not find the answer, but we can discover *how* to meet it. Christ will help us meet it, face it, and handle it. Our guilt? He comes to help us face that, too. He comes to offer us forgiveness. He's willing to take guilt away from us. Our burdens and cares? He knows all about them. He's carried them Himself and He will come in the midst of them to give us strength. His requirements and demands? He asks nothing of us He will ask us to do alone. He will help us meet the requirements He asks of us.

We need to understand that God is not our enemy. He is our friend working on our behalf to help us achieve the highest in life. When I was in high school, we had a principal who frightened everyone. He was known for his discipline. One day I got a call to go to the principal's office, and I did not look forward to that at all. All sorts of pictures of evil things he might do to me flooded my mind. I didn't know what I had done, but I'm sure that I had done something terrible to be called to his office. To my surprise, the principal had called me there to give me encouragement in my vocational choice. He had heard that I was going to enter the ministry, and he called me down to tell me that he thought it was a tremendous thing to do. He supported me and wanted to help me in any way he could. From that moment on, I had a new viewpoint of the principal. No longer was he someone to fear, but he was someone who was caring, compassionate, and sensitive.

Christ has shown us that this is the nature of God—caring, compassionate, forgiving, a God who is for us. We need to hear that truth again and again.

II. The ascension emphasizes Christ' desire to forgive us of our sins.

Christ is likened to a priest who made a sacrifice in behalf of the people. Christ came to do that for us, to intercede for us on behalf of God. Imagine a courtroom scene: we're condemned, we're guilty, and no one is there to speak on our behalf. Then Christ comes to speak a good word for our defense. He knows us and loves us; He has sacrificed for us, and He will tell the Judge that He has paid the penalty for our judgment, our crime. We are set free, if we're His. Christ has been our Intercessor, and He is always that—pulling for us, praying for us, waiting to step in and take away our sins. He always stands ready to plead for us.

But there is a condition, as there always is. We must be willing to give our lives over to His care. We must want Him to forgive us; we must seriously seek His forgiveness. If we do that, He stands ready to speak the good word in our behalf. Each of us is responsible to God for how we live. This is part of what the doctrine of the priesthood of believers means. When I come to judgment day, Christ will not ask *you* whether or not I have lived the kind of life that should enable me to be part of the Kingdom. He will not ask me whether *you* should be allowed into the Kingdom. He will know. For each one of us is responsible to live our lives under His leadership, under His guidance. He knows how we have done. My own feeling is that it is easier to live a life that pleases others than it is to live the life that pleases God. But this is what I must do, this is what you must do. Each of us is responsible to live our lives under His leadership.

That's a dreadful thought because no one lives a perfect life. No one will ever live free of sin. We will make our mistakes. We will fail and we will fall, but the good news of the gospel is that Christ knows this and loves us still. He knows our intentions, He knows where our heart lies, and He is willing to forgive us over and over again. He is willing to speak that good word for us. He is willing to give us that tremendous mercy.

Dr. Wilford Grenfell was asked what motivated him to give his life to Christian missions. He said that as a young man he was a resident physician in a hospital when they brought in a woman who was terribly burned. There was absolutely no hope for her. Her husband had come home drunk and had thrown a paraffin lamp over her. The police brought the half-sober husband to the hospital. The magistrate leaned over the dying woman and insisted she tell the police exactly what had happened. He told her it was important to tell the whole truth because she was going to die. The woman avoided looking at her husband, but finally she turned, and their eyes met. For a moment it seemed she no longer suffered as tenderness and love colored her countenance, then she looked at the magistrate and said, "Sir, it was just an accident," and she fell down back on the pillow and died. Dr. Grenfell said, "This was like God, and God is like that. His love sees through our sins."[2] The ascension reminds us how much God is waiting, hoping to forgive our sins.

III. The ascension emphasizes the unstoppable sovereignty of God.

Christ is the Priest forever. Nothing can take away His priesthood. He is eternal. He is above the heavens. Nothing that anyone can think of can destroy Him, not sorrow, sickness, suffering, or death. This Priest will keep His faithful children forever. There is nothing in this world or beyond it that can ever separate us from

His love. He is sovereign forever and ever. The ascension is a reminder of the tremendous unlimitedness of God. We cannot capture Him, control Him, or defeat Him.

J. B. Phillips in his book, *Your God Is Too Small,* talked about the fact that we try to get God down to our size, but it cannot be done. Sometimes we try to pin God down to space. Titov, the Russian cosmonaut, came back from his trip into space and said, "I proved there is no God because I was up there and didn't see Him." But where did He expect to find God anyway, sitting over on some planet? God is bigger than space; He is exalted above the heavens. The greatness of the universe, with its galaxies and galaxy upon galaxies—He is above all of that!

One can't contain God in space, nor can we pin Him down into ideas and words. We can't put God down in a creed, a hymn, formula, or even a complete sentence. He's greater than that. We've got to have greater thoughts about God than can be put into human words. In Texas there was a person who wanted to be rebaptized because she couldn't remember whether she was baptized "in" the name of the Lord or "by" the name of the Lord. Listen! God is not the God of a preposition. He is greater than that. We must not limit God to our human words.

Nor can we pin God down to our own wants. Sometimes we have a picture of God who's like a Santa Claus who will give us what we want and live up to our expectations. If He doesn't, we throw Him out into the wastebasket with other worn-out ideas.

We'd better take another look at what God is like. God is so great that He cannot be contained. He always was and always will be. He's Alpha and Omega, the beginning and never-ending end. He is sovereign, above the world and all the evils that dwell in it. There is nothing He cannot defeat. No suffering, no sickness, no death has ultimate power over Him. The ascension reminds us that Christ is a triumphant Christ, on the throne always, and those of us that are His—who hold on to Him—will one day celebrate the victory that He has promised us. Someone was expressing their disbelief in God and said that when one looks at the facts of the world, how can anybody believe in God? All I could say to him is that all the facts are not in yet. There's one fact that we, who are in the faith, believe with every ounce of faith in us: when all the facts are in, only Christ will be triumphant!

The story of the ascension may seem to be a strange and outdated story tucked away in the pages of the Bible, but it is a story that has meaning for us today. It reminds us that the shape of God is love, that every one of us is loved by Him, that every one of us can be forgiven by Him, and that, when we trust Him, every one of us will share unbroken fellowship with Him forever and forever. The ascension helps us to keep life and truth in perspective. It reminds us of our hope; it reminds us of our destiny.

At the funeral of Louis XIV the great Cathedral was literally packed with mourners who had come to pay their final tribute. The room was dark except for one lone candle which illuminated the gold casket holding the remains of the king. At the appointed time, Massilion, the court preacher, stood to address the assembled citizens of France. As he rose, he reached from his pulpit and snuffed out the one candle which had been put there alone to symbolize the greatness of the king. Then from the darkness came just four words, "God only is great."[3]

We need to remember that; we need to live remembering that. We need to continue to give ourselves to this God who *only* is great and will be forever.

Notes

1. George L. Earnshaw, Jr., "Running Away from Duty," *Pulpit Digest* (January 1958): 40.

2. Ruby H. Thomas, "Love Without Cause," *The New Pulpit Digest* (March-April 1973): 30.

3. Homer J. R. Elford, "How to Keep Lent," *Pulpit Preaching,* January 1971, 9.

12
Stewardship Sunday:
Climbing Up the Giving Ladder

(2 Cor. 9:7)

How many times have we heard, "You need to grow up"? Probably more than we want to. In a sense, this is what life is all about. Life is a process of growth from beginning to the end. As soon as we are born, if we do not grow physically, we will die. The same is true in all areas of our life: mentally, emotionally, and spiritually. We need to be continually growing up. There's nothing sadder to see than an adult who acts like a teenager, or a teenager who acts like a four- or five-year-old.

The same is true in the area of our discipleship. We sing that "Every day with Jesus is to be sweeter than the day before." Is this the way it is with us? It isn't with many. It is a sad picture when people come and accept Christ, and then never do anything about it, just staying the same as they were from that moment on. They never seek to deepen their prayer life, service life, or worship life. They stay the same. It's not meant to be that way. Stunted growth is not a virtue of Christian discipleship.

Paul told this to the church at Corinth, a church with feuding members, picking at each other over inconsequentials. Paul said to them, "You need to grow up." He said, "When I was a child, I spoke like a child, I thought like a child, I reasoned like a child; when I became a man, I gave up childish ways" (1 Cor. 13:11). In other words, he said to them, "Quit acting like babies! Grow up!"

That's a word that many church people still need to hear. He went on to apply that in their giving. You might say, "Uh-oh, this is that Sunday in the church when he talks about money." You're right, but let's face the simple truth: the church depends on the monetary contributions of those who are part of it. If you don't give, we can't do the ministries we need to do. The more you give, the more we can do. The truth is that we need to do a lot of growing in our stewardship. We need to do something about growing up in the area of giving. In this passage, Paul talked about it. He gave what I call a "ladder of giving," certain stages of giving that we can go through. Now, I am assuming that everybody understands and wants to at least give. We know that we need to give so that the cause of Christ can be spread. There are certain ways we can give as we grow to be the kind of giver we need to be. What kind of giver are we?

I. For instance, the first rung of this ladder is that some people give grudgingly.

Paul said, don't give "relunctantly." Evidently, some people were giving who didn't want to give. They didn't see why they had to support the ministry of Paul or that of the early church. Their attitude was, "Do I have to?" They gave, but when they gave, they gave with a groan because they really didn't want to. It was a pain for them to give.

I can identify with that because there was a time in my life when this was the way it was for me. When I grew up my parents wanted to teach me to be a tither, so they made me tithe all that I made from my allowance, my paper route, and odd jobs. I remember telling them one time, "Do I have to?" I can't quite tell you the answer they gave me, but I gave. I didn't see why I had to give my hard-earned money to the church budget. True, I believed in God, I enjoyed the activities that the church did, and I liked the preacher and the people in it, but just why did I have to give my money?

Can you identify with that? Maybe this is the way you are now. A bumper sticker said, "God loveth a cheerful giver, but He also taketh from a grouch." But I'm not too sure that's true. Do you enjoy getting a gift from somebody who you know really didn't want to give it to you and complained about it? When people give you gifts like that, you have a tendency to want to throw it right back at them and say, "Keep it!" Sometimes this is the way we give to God. Remember, God might be saying the same thing to us, "Take it back because you don't mean it."

There was a movie I saw on television starring Burt Reynolds called *The End.* The man played by Reynolds thought he had a dreaded, serious disease, so he wanted to find a way to commit suicide. He went out into the ocean once, waded out into the deep water, thinking about drowning himself. While there, the revelation hit him that he didn't want to die, he wanted to live. He looked way to the shore far in the distance, and he looked up to God and said, "God, if you get me back to shore, I'll give you 90 percent of all that I have." So the man began to swim back to shore, and he got closer. He then said, "God, if I get back to shore, I'll give you 60 percent of all that I own." He got closer, 30 percent, closer, "Are we talking net or gross?" Finally, when the man got to the shore, he looked up to God and said, "Well, after all, You got me into this mess." Off he ran down the beach, and we laughed at it. Sort of funny, wasn't it? But it's really a sad picture of somebody maybe who thinks he can put one over on God, as if God's a dummy. But the movie character was someone who didn't care that much about God, didn't care about giving Him a thing, only getting what he could get out of Him.

Often we give and complain about giving. Inside, what we are saying is that we don't really care about Him. We need to grow out of that. If this is you, if you give with a moan and a groan, you need to move up to the second rung of this ladder.

II. We can give out of a sense of obligation.

Paul said not to give out of "compulsion." Evidently, some were doing that. There were those who were giving because they felt they had to. They gave not out of joy, but out of obligation and duty. They didn't say, "Do I have to?" They knew they needed to. They were saying instead, "OK, I ought to." But at the same time, they did not feel the joy inside they should have felt in giving to the ministries of God. Maybe they gave out of a sense of guilt. Maybe their parents taught them to give. Maybe they gave out of pressure. They gave, but out of duty, not love.

A lot of us may be giving out of a sense of duty. We know the church needs it. We know we need to do it, but we don't enjoy it at all. It's an obligation, something that hangs over our heads. I understand this because I had that, too. When I was in seminary, I went through my rebellious period as far as giving was concerned. I said, "After all, I'm giving my whole life to the ministry of Christ and going through seminary is not easy." We didn't have all that much money, so why should I have to give? At the same time, I knew that Christians should be givers, and those who were going to be ministers ought to be good givers. So I gave, but at the same time, I didn't enjoy it. It was something I did because I ought to, but not something I enjoyed.

Do you enjoy giving, or is giving an obligation to you? We need to take our responsibilities seriously, and there are obligations and ministries of the church we need to perform. But to give to the church out of a sense of duty rather than love doesn't bring any of us what it ought to bring. I'm not sure how much God enjoys that kind of giving, either, giving just because we ought to, not really because we're glad to. There isn't much inner satisfaction in that.

I heard about a man who was leading a fund-raising campaign for a new building for his church. On a certain day people came, made pledges, and gave money. There were lots of rich people in that particular church. One man came up and said, "I'm going to give a thousand dollars," and the people applauded. Somebody else got up and said, "I'm going to give five hundred" and the people applauded. Another man said, "I'm going to give two thousand," and the people applauded. One of the women got up in ragged clothes and said, "I'm going to give ten dollars." Nobody applauded. The minister said, "I think we all need to be quiet, for I think I hear applause from the nail-scarred hands." Somebody giving, not because they had to, but because they wanted to. This leads to the third rung of the ladder.

III. "God loves a cheerful giver."

Now that word *cheerful* means "hilarious." The picture was people who just couldn't contain the joy of being able to give to God. They just loved to give to God. They were glad to give to God, they just bubbled over because they had a chance to give to God. They gave to God because of what God had done for them, because they loved Him and knew God was going to provide for their needs. They trusted God to take care of them. As Paul said, Whoever "sows bountifully will also reap bountifully." They didn't bother to worry about whether or not they would make it. They trusted God to take care of them. They just were booming over with joy at being able to give.

Have you found many people like that? I have talked to a lot of folks in the church about giving. Many ask, "Do I have to tithe the net or the gross?" To me, it seems that many people are trying to say, "How little do I have to give?" I never run into many who say, "How much can I give?" I'd love to run into some folks like that. "How much can I give?" This is what God loves, a hilarious, cheerful giver, glad to give, wanting to give, trusting God to take care of them when they give. This might be the question of our stewardship. Do we believe that if we give sacrificially, maybe more than we've ever done before, that we will be able to survive? Do we feel that if we give, God will be able to provide for our needs? I wonder what would happen if we did that? All of us believe that God will keep His word, and He will provide for our needs—not our luxuries—but our needs. What would happen if instead of trying to figure out how little can we give, we can think about how much? I wonder if the joy would begin to come. To do the work of Christ through the church, we need to be that kind of giver.

A church had a very beautiful organ donated by one of its members. But there was one problem. Whenever things in the church didn't go the way she wanted, early on Sunday mornings she would sit at that organ, and not let anybody else play it. They would go to play, and she would be sitting there with the threat, "Push me off." Of course, nobody wanted to do her any physical harm, so there she sat through the service on a gift she had given. The moral: when we sit on our gifts, the music stops.[1] If we sit on our giving, the music will stop throughout the church in some of the ways we need it. But if we are cheerful givers, the music goes on.

In other words, when you give, you will help provide for buildings, materials, equipment, staff, and leadership to give a witness in your community for Christ through His church. When you give, you will help witness for Christ around this world through missionaries. When you give, you will help find homes for orphans and abused children where people will care for them. When you give, you will help provide education for people in seminaries who will lead churches in the days ahead. When you give, you will provide sick people places where they can find doctors and nurses who can minister to them. When you give, you will help feed the hungry. When you give, you will help minister to people everywhere.

It is exciting to think the money we give can be used to invest in people's lives, that maybe what we give will be used to bring light to somebody's darkness, food to somebody who is hungry, or ease the pain of somebody's hurts. What we do may bring somebody the Light of the world, and the music will go on. To know we're giving to that ought to cause us to feel good about it, to want to give gladly—not grudgingly, not out of duty—but out of joy knowing that it is going to do all that.

The attitude of the cheerful giver is: "I want to give. I'm glad to give. I'm happy to give." Is this where you are? This is the goal of our growth in stewardship: to move beyond the moaning, groaning, and sense of obligation to the joy, gladness, and hilarity that comes from giving. What God promises us is that, if we live joyfully, He will reward us joyfully.

Note

1. Clara Bing Binford, "The Crazies," *The Clergy Journal* (October 1979): 9-10.

13
Stewardship Sunday:
The Unforgettable Gift

(Mark 12:41-44)

Have you ever received an unforgettable gift? I remember one I received when I was a youngster. A pet cat died and at my tender age, that was quite traumatic. I didn't think I could ever make it through that moment. But the next day my parents took a ride out into the country and invited me to go along. We stopped at a farmhouse and went to the barn. In the barn was a cat with seven or eight kittens running around her. That was a joy for me to see. An even greater joy came when my parents said to me, "Pick one out, and we'll take it home with us." Of all the many gifts I have received in my life, that one was unforgettable. I needed it. It helped me through a very difficult time.

Have you ever received an unforgettable gift? You have probably received many of them. But let me ask you this, have you ever given one? I think it is a precious gift to be able to give to someone what they need at the right moment, a gift that will never be forgotten because of what it meant to them. Maybe it was some thing they needed, a shoulder to cry on, a helping hand, or an encouraging word; but it was a gift you were able to bestow on them, and they have never forgotten it.

I want to tell you about a way you can give an unforgettable gift now. You have probably guessed that my subject is stewardship: I'm going to talk about money. Talk about it I must, for it is a very important part of discipleship. It was so important that Jesus talked about our relationship to material possessions more than He did anything else. Being a practical person, we must face up to the price tag for ministry for Christ in the church. I want to try to get behind the cold "dollar-and-cents" facts to try to understand what it is all about, to help us understand that when we give to the ministry of Christ, we're giving an unforgettable gift, one that He'll never forget, and because He will never forget, neither will those whose lives He is able to touch through our gifts.

The text is the story of the poor widow who stood before the church treasury with her paltry sum. Others around her were giving great amounts, and she had so little to give, but give it she did. Of all the gifts given that day, Jesus remembered hers. It was, for Him, the unforgettable gift. What caused it to be unforgettable? What can we do to make sure what we give is unforgettable?

I. An unforgettable gift is given out of grateful love.

We get the picture here of a woman who was in a struggle. People around her were giving great sums, perhaps to the applause of the watching crowd. Whenever they put in a great sum, it made a big noise that sounded like a trumpet blowing. The people would say, "My, what a great amount you have given! You must truly be religious." But all this widow had was a pauper's sum, maybe a penny or two, and she struggled about whether or not to give it. If she threw it in, the crowd might laugh at her. She might be embarrassed by what she gave in comparison to others. Finally, the struggle ended, and she tossed in her little sum. Jesus saw it and said, "She has put in everything."

What caused her to give it? She was in a difficult situation. She was a widow. She had known what it was to go through the grief of losing a husband. She was poor, which probably meant that she had little family, that she had been left on her own to survive. But she gave everything she had: Why? Maybe because she had lost almost everything, except her faith in God. She still believed in Him. She still was grateful for all He had been and done for her.

She still loved Him. In spite of all her need, her pain, in gratitude and love for what He was, she threw in all she had.

When all is said and done, there is no higher motive for giving than this: we give because we are thankful to God for what He has done for us. We give because we love Him. It's a whole lot easier to give to somebody we love, isn't it? The idea of giving in the Christian faith is "hilarious" giving, giving that's joyful because we love the God to whom we give. There's only one reason you don't need to make a commitment to stewardship and that is this: God has never done anything for you. If you have never had any of your sins forgiven, if you have never been uplifted in the service of worship, if you have never found inner strength to go through difficult moments, if you have never been loved by fellow Christians, if you have never known the beauty of sunrise and sunset, if you have never been encouraged by the hope of eternal life, then you have no reason to give. But if any of these blessings have ever come your way, then how lucky you are, how blessed you are. We don't deserve the blessings of God, but they come over and over again. In thanksgiving for what He's done for us, we give.

People give from all sorts of motives. The only worthy one I know is to point people's lives to what happened on the cross of Christ. If what He did for us there—if what He did for YOU there—does not *mean* anything to you, there is nothing I can ever say that will. It is His love that ought to be the cause of all of our giving. When you think of it, how can we *not* give?

A friend told me about a teacher who was given the assignment of working with a very difficult young girl. Many had tried to work with this girl, but without success. She was trouble from the word *go.* She would rebel against everything and did so with this new teacher. The teacher tried everything she knew to reach her. The teacher struggled with the child, was patient with her, went places with her, but never thought she was getting anyplace with her.

One day the teacher came into class and saw a little envelope on the desk. She opened it. It was a handmade card. The picture on it was not well drawn, the letters were not well formed, and the card simply said, "I love you." It was from this girl that the teacher could not reach. The teacher said, "Of all of the gifts that I have ever gotten through the years, the one that stands central on my shelf is that little handmade card." Ugly to look at, words written very carelessly—"I love you." But that gift was unforgettable, for it meant all the love she had poured into the girl was not wasted. Some of it had gotten through.

I hope all of the love God has thrown at us has not been wasted. One way we can show Him it has not been wasted is through our material gifts.

II. An unforgettable gift is also sacrificial.

All of these people gave, Jesus said, "out of their abundance." In other words, they didn't miss it. When they gave, it was not really hard for them. Here was a widow who gave everything she had, her whole living. For her to give was sacrifice upon sacrifice. Jesus saw it, admired it, respected it, and remembered it. The gift was sacrificial.

Whenever we come to make our commitments of stewardship to Christ, they ought to be sacrificial. I read of a couple of kids left at home one day who wanted to play a game, so they decided to play what they had heard in Sunday School. They would be Mr. and Mrs. Noah. They got a cardboard box and went into the bathtub, put the plug into the bathtub, and turned on the shower. That was the sign of the flood! They put all of the animals into the cardboard box, and the box rose up. They stopped the shower and pulled the plug as a sign that the flood was over.

They had a good time, but they had a problem. At the end of the story, the Bible said that Noah offered a sacrifice to God. They asked, "What can we do to offer a sacrifice to God?" The little girl said, "I know." She reached over and took one of her brother's animals. "We'll sacrifice this one." The brother said, "Oh, no, you won't! I want that. I know, we can sacrifice this." He reached over and got one of the sister's animals. "No, you don't. I want that!" They thought for a moment. The sister said, "I've got an idea." She ran upstairs, went through some old toys, and brought down a toy sheep that had only three legs; the tail was gone, and the head was smashed in. She said, "We can sacrifice this because we don't need it anymore."[1]

How many give God that kind of stewardship? We give what we don't miss, what we don't need. The giving is never hurtful. Does it hurt you to give? Does it cost to give? What do you give up because you give to the cause of Christ through the church? Anything? As someone said, and I think rightly, "Until it hurts to give, you never know what it is to give."

Dr. George W. Truett, that great Texas Baptist preacher, was invited many years ago to a church which was raising funds to dedicate a new church building. As the pledges had barely passed the halfway mark, they ceased. Then, Dr. Truett said, a plainly dressed woman arose and spoke to her husband, who had been recording the pledges, "Charley," she said, "I wonder if you would be willing to give our little home, just out of debt. Just yesterday we were offered enough for it to push us over our goal. Would you be willing to give our little house for Christ that this house may be free?" Her fine husband responded in the same high spirit, "Jennie, dear, I was thinking the same thing." Then looking up at Dr. Truett with his face covered with tears, he said, "We will give the rest!"

There followed a scene which cannot be described. Men and women sobbed aloud and almost in a moment the rest of the goal was reached. And then, without an invitation being given, men and women came down the aisle saying, "Sir, where is the Savior? How can we find Him?"[2]

That's sort of weird, isn't it? People would do *that!* We don't hear too much of that kind of giving anymore, but that's the kind of gift God remembers and blesses. That's what real giving means, that we'd rather have Jesus than anything. When it comes to stewardship, we don't say, "I wish I didn't have to give it." We say instead, "I'm glad I can." Stewardship is sacrificial. God never forgets that kind of gift.

III. An unforgettable gift is surprising in what it can do.

This woman never thought that what she gave could make a difference. It was so little. Jesus saw it, remembered it, and used it as an example of what true giving meant. Down through the years, many have been inspired to deeper stewardship through her example. Two thousand years later, we still remember her act. I'm hoping that because of what she did we will reexamine our own stewardship to see if we do as well. She gave just a little tiny gift. Compared to all the rest, it seemed so small. But it wasn't the amount, it was the commitment behind it. Jesus was able to take it and use that gift in surprising ways.

He always can and does. What we give, if we give sacrificially from a heart of grateful love, Christ can take and use in ways we cannot even imagine. There was a girl who went to Sunday School in Philadelphia. The building was overcrowded. They didn't have any room for her. She was disturbed about that. She felt they needed to build a bigger church, so they could have room for everybody, and she started saving her pennies. Unfortunately, the little girl died. They found under her pillow 57 pennies with a little note telling why she was saving the pennies. They read that note at her funeral. It got into the newspaper and was the beginning of the inspiration for many gifts coming in through the mail. That 57 cents multiplied to $250,000. From those gifts the Baptist Temple of Philadelphia, the Good Samaritan Hospital, and Temple University in Philadelphia were begun. All from the love of a little girl who gave 57 cents.[3] Who could have thought or believed that such a little sum could lead to so much?

This is the way God works. He takes our little and uses it in magnificent ways. If it's from a heart of love, if it's from a heart willing to sacrifice, He blesses it, and others are blessed. Remember that children's favorite, Stone Soup? The story tells of hungry soldiers who go into a town looking for food. They get a huge kettle, fill it with water, select a large stone, throw that in the pot, build a fire under the kettle, and begin to stir. The curious townspeople ask what the soldiers are doing. "Making Stone Soup," they declare. "This soup is delicious, but a little cabbage would make it better." One villager says, "I have some cabbage you can have." He goes into his storeroom and brings a cabbage. Item by item, the soldiers tell the curious villagers what will make the soup better; a few carrots, celery, turnips, potatoes, onions, some salt, and parsley. One by one the items are brought forth. Finally, the soldiers announce that a piece of meat would make the soup exquisite, and a family brings forth that hidden treasure. Indeed, the soup was exquisite. All had invested the little they had, and there was plenty of everything for all.[4]

Will we give an unforgettable gift to God? He waits to see. Others wait to see. What will we do? Bruce Larson, in his book: *Believe and Belong*, told about a very wealthy Christian businessman who was asked back to his home church to speak to the Sunday School class he had attended long years ago. The children were curious about this man now worth millions and asked him to tell how it all began. He said, "Well, it all began right here in this church. Those were hard times. I was a young man with no job and very poor. We had a guest preacher who said, 'Give your life and all that you have to Jesus, and He will bless you.' I had $3.34 in my pocket. It was all that I had in the world, and I put the whole thing in the plate. I gave my life to the Lord that day, and He has blessed me ever since." He closed his talk with a time for questions, and the first hand up was that of a little boy in the front row. "Mister," he said, "Could you do it now?"[5]

Will we do it now?

Notes

1. Julius King, *Successful Fund-Raising* (New York: Funk & Wagnalls Company, 1953), 59-60.

2. Michael Fink, "A Gift Remembered—A Name Forgotten," *Award-Winning Sermons,* vol. 2 (Nashville: Broadman Press, 1978), 133.

3. C. Thomas Hilton, "The Dead Still Speak," *The Clergy Journal* (October 1980): 13.

4. *Pulpit Resource* (October, November, December 1981): 24.

5. *Pastor's Professional Research Service,* July 1986, 19.

14
Mission Sunday:
The Mission Before Us

(Mark 10:17-22)

I received a phone call from an excited young man. He had just become the father of a new baby girl and was bubbling over with excitement. He just had to call me and tell me about it. At a religious convention, I ran across a preacher friend. He was excited because he had been called to another church. He was thrilled about the possibilities and opportunities of the new work. All he could talk about the whole week was what was going to happen in the days ahead. I got a letter from an old friend who wrote about a significant job promotion. It was a great career move for him, and he wanted to share his exciting good news.

All of these people had good news to share and they just had to tell somebody. In its simplest definition, this is what missions, witnessing, and evangelism are. It is sharing the good news that has happened to us. We just have to tell somebody what Christ has done for us and is doing for us. This is missions and we need to be doing it. Christ has come to be where we are. He has brought us love and forgiveness and hope and life. That's the greatest news we have ever heard. What we need to do is to share it.

During Christmas in the Southern Baptist Convention the Lottie Moon Offering for Foreign Missions is taken. Lottie Moon was a missionary who gave her life in China. She died on Christmas Eve. That's why the offering is held at Christmas—to honor her memory. It is a good thing to do for, when we talk about giving and receiving gifts, the best gift we can give anybody is what we have received from Christ. We need to do this for, if we do not share the gospel, then the faith will die. If churches are not mission-minded, we will suffer. We will have no reason to exist if we are not interested in sharing the gospel through missions.

This Scripture told of Jesus meeting the rich young man. In that experience, we can get some insight into missions, how Jesus did His mission work, and what that means for us.

I. The motivation for our mission: love for others.

This text says, "Jesus looking upon him loved him" (v. 21). That is not surprising, for this was what Jesus was always doing—loving people. This was why He came. "For God so loved the world"—that means you and me. Everywhere Jesus went, He helped people because He loved them. He wanted to share with them what He had to give.

This is the only reason we should do anything for Christ, out of love for Him which leads to love for others. If we care about people, we want to share with them the best things we have. Here is a child who is sick. Nobody can learn what is the matter with her. You know what is wrong. You have the medicine she needs. Because you care for her, you will give her the medicine so she can live. If you don't give her the medicine, then people will say that you do not care, that she means nothing to you. In the same sense, all across this world there are many who are dying spiritually. Their lives are in a mess. They have no hope, joy, or peace inside. They are restless and lost because they have not found the cure for it. They have not given themselves away to the Giver of life. We have the cure. We know the answer, and, if we do not give it away, then we do not care. We must share the gospel so people can hear it and live.

A church in Sacramento, Kentucky, in the Cumberland Gap, was small, with 130 members, a budget of $12,000 a year, and a part-time pastor. They felt that they couldn't do much in missions. But they began to have a conviction that they needed to be concerned about foreign missions. Four of them, three farmers and a boilermaker, went for a period of time to serve in the Sudan. They went to put a boiler in a hospital. The boiler had been there for three years, but nobody knew how to put it in. After they put the boiler in, they found tractors that didn't work, so they took parts from three of them and made one tractor work. They found some other things they could do as they ministered in the name of Christ. When they went back, they went speaking about the needs of missions. They raised $5,000 to send needed supplies. The next year, others went to Colombia to serve with the poor. They were a tiny church with the world on their hearts, and they became a church alive. Their budget grew from $12,000 to $39,000. They grew in membership, got a full-time pastor, and it all came about because they became concerned enough to share the gospel everywhere.[1]

If ever we quit caring about what happens in Christ's name in Africa, or in South America, or anywhere, it will be tragic. Our spirits will shrivel up; our faith will become weak.

II. The message: Christ can meet their needs.

Missions is to share Christ and how He can meet people's needs. Jesus answered this man's question: "What must I do to inherit eternal life?" He told the young ruler that he loved his money more than he did God. If he wanted to find eternal life, he had to give up his love of money. Jesus told him to go and sell what he had, then come and follow Him. If he did that, then his needs would be met. Jesus told him what he needed to hear to be free.

That's what missions is: telling how Jesus can meet their needs. He can free them from their sins or whatever it is that has control of their lives. We think that to do missions we've got to learn all the Scriptures. To witness, we learn methods to go out and tell somebody about the faith. What we learn is good, and what we learn of Scripture is good, but witnessing, missions, and evangelism is simply telling somebody else what *you* know about Christ.

What has happened to you? How has Christ helped you? What has Christ meant to you? What has Christ done for you? That's what we tell, for we ought to have a story, a story about how Christ has come into our lives, brought us joy and peace, and freed us from our guilt and shame. Christ has come to us, forgiven us, and given us a reason to live. He has met our needs. Missions is going across the world telling the story that Jesus Christ can save them from whatever it is that keeps them from being free to live.

An airman was shot down in the South Seas and landed on an island he had heard a lot about. It was one of those unknown islands in the Pacific. Cannibals supposedly were there, and nobody ever got out alive. He hid in the bushes, but he was found. The pilot was surprised by what he found. It was a tribe at peace. They had no sheriff and no jail because they had no crimes. They had no divorce. They had one doctor, but he spent most of the time fishing. There were no arguments. Whenever a child was orphaned another family automatically took the child in. They cared for one another. The airman could not believe it. He asked, "What's the secret? How can you live in such harmony and peace?" The chief of the tribe said, "You ought to know. You sent us the missionaries who told us how we could have it. They told us about Christ, and we've taken Him seriously."[2]

Christ can change people. He can change communities. He can change churches. Christ has the power to meet our needs and make us new. That's the message we have to tell all the nations.

III. The manner of our missions: complete trust and dependence on God for what happens.

After Jesus told the rich young ruler what he had to do, the Scripture says, "He went away sorrowful; for he had great possessions" (v. 22). It seemed that Jesus failed. He didn't win this person to the faith. Some have suggested that what He should have done was to go after the man to talk some more. But Jesus did what He had to do. Jesus told him the truth, what he needed to do. Then

He left it there because it was up to the man to respond to the truth. Jesus trusted God with what happened after that. Did the young man ever become part of the Kingdom? We don't know. The opportunity was his, but it was his alone to choose.

We need to understand that we have the responsibility to tell the truth, to preach the gospel, and offer it to people; but then we must learn to depend upon God for what happens after that. We are seed planters; we must trust God for the bloom and the flower. Sometimes we get frustrated when we try to lead people to Christ, and nobody seems to respond. Adonirom Judson worked for seven years without a single convert in Burma. He felt like he was a failure, but he wasn't. He wasn't because he did what he was supposed to do. He witnessed to the faith; he told his story. In the end, God's presence was discovered to work among them.

We plant; God brings the flower. God works and sometimes has a way of working in lives that defy our imagination. A boy was asked in a church in England to give a penny to missions. The boy was skeptical; he didn't see how giving a penny was going to help anybody. So the preacher made a deal with him. Give the penny, and the preacher would give him a Bible. "I'll give you the name and address of a missionary in India, and I want you to send that Bible to him." The boy said, "OK," and gave the preacher the penny. He wrote an inscription on the fly leaf and sent it to a missionary in India. That missionary in India gave it to an English-speaking Indian who had walked several miles to see him. The Indian was a believer and was trying to get the missionary to come to some of the villages, but the missionary could not go. The Indian got the Bible and went back into the jungle. Twenty years later, another missionary finally made it back to that area where nobody had ever been to preach the gospel. When he got there, he found that village after village were Christian communities. In trying to find out why, the missionary discovered that the English-speaking Indian, to whom the Bible had been given, had gone back into those areas and begun reading the Bible, interpreting it to the people. Christian communities sprang up all over that area because a boy gave a penny that enabled a Bible to be sent and to be given to God's use.[3]

That's missions! That boy had a great deal to do with starting those Christian communities in India. He never went. He gave what he could. God took it up from there. Do we believe that can happen? We need to do the best we can to tell the truth and then let God take it from that moment on.

That is our mission: to do what we can to share the story of Christ in order to help others. A medical missionary told of a woman who came to see him. She'd walked 100 miles to catch a train, then went another 200 miles. She brought her child. He had diptheria. The missionary thought it was too late for the child, but with a tracheotomy and a little medicine, the child got better. Then the mother said, "Can you look at me?" It was discovered that she had breast cancer, so the missionary doctor did surgery on her, and her life was saved. Someone asked him later, "What do you think these medical supplies cost?" "The supplies to help that little boy cost $4.67. The supplies used to help that woman cost $16.50, so that makes twenty-one dollars and seventeen cents. But for that money two lives were saved in the name of Christ."[4]

How many lives will be touched by what we give also? Somebody believed in missions enough to go to a place that needed a medical missionary. Somebody believed in missions enough to send money to support the work. God used their gifts, and His love was seen. That is the mission before us. To go and do it. To support others who do it. To trust God to bless the work. For He always will.

Notes

1. John Killinger, "The Healthiest Church in the World," sermon at First Presbyterian Church, Lynchburg, Virginia, 1 March 1981, 5-6.

2. Leslie Weatherhead, "Does God Matter?, *Pulpit Digest* (December 1959): 38.

3. Leslie Weatherhead, *Key Next Door* (New York: Abingdon Press, 1959-1960), 206.

4. Raymond E. Balcomb, "A Well, a Tent, and an Altar," *Pulpit Digest* (November 1957): 22.

15
Communion Sunday:
Understanding the Supper—
Knowing Its Names

(2 Cor. 11:23-26)

Do you understand the meaning of the Lord's Supper? Unfortunately there is a lot of misunderstanding about it. Down through the years argument over this particular celebration has been a bone of contention between religious groups. It has led to furious debate and fractured fellowships. It's a tragedy that what God intended to be a reminder of what we have in common has often been a reminder of what separates us.

Do we understand it? If someone came up to you and asked you to explain the meaning and significance of it, what would you tell them? Who is this for? What does it mean? What is supposed to happen to us because we go through it? Can you answer those questions? We need to have an understanding of what we do when we celebrate this in our worship experience. What I want to do is help us understand its meaning by sharing with you the four names by which it is known. If we know these names, it will help us as we seek to explain the meaning of it to others.

I. It is known as the Lord's Supper.

This is the name that I prefer and use more than any other. I like it because it reminds us, for one thing, that it is the *Lord's* Supper. He is the one who brought this into being. It was on the night in the upper room, after they had eaten the Passover meal that celebrated their deliverance from slavery in Egypt, that Jesus added this part: He took the bread, He took the cup, and He said, "Do this in remembrance of Me." This Supper was not the creation of any church. It was not the idea of any man or denomination. The Supper was created by Christ for every one of us. He is the One who started it. He is the One who offered the invitation to it.

That is why I do not believe in what is often called "closed communion," an idea that only those who are members of a particular local church can celebrate in the Communion. It is not the church's supper, it is Christ's. He is the One who does the inviting, and His invitation is to whosoever will believe. This supper is for all who believe in Christ as Savior and Lord. Believers are invited to come and participate.

The Lord's Supper is also a symbol of what He has done for us. He said, "Do this in remembrance of Me." That's a key phrase in our understanding of the Supper. He set this apart to aid our memory because it would be easy to forget, with all that goes on in life, just exactly what the heart of the gospel is about. The Supper is to remind us of what Christ did. It is a symbol, a signpost, something that prods our imagination, and causes us to think of another reality. The danger often is that the symbol sometimes comes to be identified with that reality, and it must not. The flag is a symbol of our country. It points to the reality of our country, but it is not our country. We must not worship the flag; we must serve the United States. The Bible is a signpost that points beyond itself to Christ. We must not fall into the habit of worshiping the Bible. Instead, we must make sure we worship the Christ the Bible points us to. These elements are symbols: bread that symbolizes His body broken on the cross; the cup that symbolizes His blood shed for us on the cross. They are symbols that point to the resurrection of Christ and His crucifixion. It reminds us that God loves us so much that He was willing to die on our behalf to give us love that we didn't deserve, forgiveness that we desperately need, and a hope of eternal life that we must have. He died on a cross to bring that about. Remember, the cross is empty. This reminds us that Christ is risen. He died on a cross and conquered it. Our sins can be forgiven, love can be known and known forever; every one of us can be part of the kingdom of God because Christ loved us so much that He was willing to have His body broken and His blood shed for every one of us.

When we come to this table, we're to remember that Christ, who died for us, rose for us because He loved us. The heart of our gospel is this death and resurrection symbolized here The Lord's Supper.

II. It is called Eucharist.

That is a strange word to us. It's how our Catholic friends describe their celebration of the Supper. It's a good word. The word means "to give thanks." To celebrate this Supper is an act of thanksgiving to God for what He has done.

Surely this is what we ought to be doing, too, as we remember all that Christ has done for us. We ought to be filled with the spirit of thanksgiving and joy when we participate. It is a way of thanking God, for He has saved us from our sins, and our lostness. In a movie called *Family Life,* a daughter, Jan, felt alienated from her parents. Her parents were decent people, but somehow their relationship was fractured. They could not communicate, could not get together. The picture portrayed Jan's misery and frustration. Once she and her boyfriend put paint all over the garden. They broke expensive furniture all through the house showing the fact that the daughter was not happy, that she felt lost, cut off.[1]

This is how we feel when we have cut ourselves off from God. We will feel frustrated, miserable, and empty inside. No matter what we do to numb the emptiness inside of us, it won't happen because we're cut off from the One we need to be at home with. What Christ has done is to remove all of the barriers that keep us from going home, all the barriers that keep us from being at one with our heavenly Parent. Every one of us can go home again. Christ has made it possible. There's no one who needs to be cut off from God because Christ has taken care of our rebellion and the consequences of it. If we want to go home to God, we can.

To remember that ought to cause us to offer praise to God, to offer thanks. That's what we do by our participation in this. We're thanking God for His willingness to offer us a chance to be His children again.

III. It is called Communion.

The Communion service is often what we call it, and that word means "to experience another," "to have a close union with another." When we commune with nature, we experience nature. When we commune with a friend, we experience friendship. When we commune with God, we experience God. We do not remember and celebrate what a dead person did. We celebrate a living presence. Because Christ rose from the dead, He is alive, and the hope of our celebration is that we will experience the presence of God in a new way inside of us.

The Scripture tells us that where two or three are gathered, He is with us (Matt. 18:20). We are two or three; therefore, the presence of God is indeed with us in this experience of worship. The hope of our worship is that we will experience in our lives that this is really Christ here, really Christ speaking to us through bread and the cup. Someone went to a worship service, and the preacher was preaching about Christ. The woman said, "It got to the place where I felt Christ had come right down the aisle and looked at me and said, 'Here am I.' " It is my belief, faith, and hope that we can experience His presence in what we do. As we remember and give thanks for what He's done, He is here reaching out to us with the same love and forgiveness He offered then. We can know it again.

IV. It is called Sacrament.

That word scares us, but it ought not to because it's a good word. *Sacrament* means "oath of allegiance." Its original meaning had to do with the oath that a Roman soldier swore at the beginning of his military service. He swore that he would serve the emperor to the death. Every now and then throughout his career, the soldier would be asked to renew his sacrament, his oath of allegiance, his pledge of loyalty.

In this supper, we remember Christ's sacrament to us. He pledged His loyalty to us to the death. He pledged to God that He would do whatever was needed in order to bring us a chance at salvation. He kept that pledge, all the way through to the death and beyond.

When we remember all that, hopefully we will renew our sacrament, our pledge of allegiance, our oath of loyalty. We made them, didn't we? When we became a Christian, we were full of all sorts of promises and pledges. We were going to be this, and we were going to do that. Sometimes in the rush and busyness of life we forget the promises we've made. But we can renew them! The experience of celebrating this Supper is supposed to do that for us. As we participate, remember, give thanks, and open ourselves up to His presence, hopefully the result of it will be that we will renew the pledges, the commitments, and the loyalties that we offered Him. We will do what we said we would do: serve Him to the end.

Sometimes a couple comes and wants to renew their vows of marriage. They made them at the beginning. However, sometimes a promise made at the beginning of marriage gets broken or forgotten, so some will come and say, "We need to renew our vows." So we enter a sanctuary and go through the vows, and they speak them to one another again, renewing their commitment to keep the promises of love. In the same sense, when we participate in this Supper, it is our way of renewing our promises of commitment, our promises of love that we have made to Him.

So we come to celebrate this Lord's Supper. He invites us to do that, to remember His sacrifice on our behalf. We celebrate this Eucharist, by giving thanks to God for doing what He did for us.

We celebrate this Communion, as we open ourselves up to the living presence of Christ who is here even now. We celebrate this Sacrament, as we renew our pledge of loyalty, devotion, and commitment to this Christ who committed Himself so to us.

There's something about the celebration of the Supper that speaks to us. It is the gospel, not only of word but for the eye. It does remind us; it opens us up to all that Christ did and was and all that He wants to be. One woman said, "Every time I celebrate the Supper, it makes me want to love Him more." I hope so, because we can't love Him too much. We need to love Him more. To remember and celebrate will lead us to do just that. Let us remember and celebrate!

Note

1. Alec Gilmore, *Tomorrow's Pulpit* (Valley Forge, Pa.: Judson Press, 1975), 33.

16
Communion Sunday:
A Time for Doxologies

(1 Thess. 5:18)

The apostle Paul told the Christians in Thessolonica, "Give thanks in all circumstances." That's easy to do sometimes. It's easy to give thanks when a baby is born, when we're sick and get well, when a child does well, or when we get a job promotion. When the sun is shining, it's not so hard to sing, "Praise God from whom all blessings flow."

There are other times when it's not so easy; for instance, when the baby cries at two o'clock in the morning because he's hungry, or we get sick, and stay sick; the child turns out badly, or we don't get that job promotion, in fact, we get fired. In those moments, it's hard to find the words to sing a doxology to God.

But Paul said, "In every thing give thanks" (KJV). In all "circumstances" give thanks, that no matter what happens to us, we can give thanks. How can we do that? Maybe this Supper can give us some indication of that, for here was something terrible, a very bad circumstance. A cross lifted on a lonely hill, a body broken and blood shed, Jesus killed. However, we come to celebrate that event today, not in despair, but in joy and in hope because we know that even in that experience, God was working. This is why we can give thanks in all circumstances because in any circumstance that happens to us, God is working in it to try to help us grow from it. He can take any circumstance and use that moment to help us become what we ought to be.

This is what this Supper is trying to tell us. God is alive and well in our world and working in it to help us. What does it mean? When are the times for doxologies?

I. We can give a doxology in difficult circumstances because God might be using that to surround us with His love.

If there's anything this tells us, it's of the intenseness of God's love for us. God created the world and put us in it to share its joy, but like rebellious children, we didn't want to live by His rules. We wanted to do it our way. We told God to get lost, and walked away from Him right into suffering, despair, emptiness, and pain. We deserved it, for that's what we chose to do. But the good news is that God did not let us stay there. Most fathers with such rebellious children would disinherit them, but not God. Instead, God came looking for His children who had turned away from Him. "Where are you, Adam?" He asked.

Down through history, that has been the cry of God coming down upon the face of the earth, crying out your name, my name, "Where are you?" He wants to find us. He wants us to come home to where we need to be. He wants us to experience the joy of His love. When He climbed the cross and died on it, it was His supreme call to every one of us, "Come home. I love you, and I want you to know that."

The Christian religion has a unique facet. In it, God comes looking for us. That's not the way it is in the other religions of the world. People have to go looking for God in those. But they will never be successful. Franz Kafka wrote in *The Castle* about a surveyor who was called to a distant town to work. The lord of the town lived in a castle on the hill, and it was hard to reach. The surveyor asked the villagers how he could reach it; and they were shocked that he wanted to go up to the castle, so they avoided him. He tried many ways to find a way up to the castle, but never could, and he died frustrated. Not only was the surveyor unable to get up to the castle, but he was not able to discover what he was supposed to do in that town.[1]

Kafka wrote *The Castle* to try to point out how difficult it was for human beings to reach God. His opinion was that we can't, that God was too far removed from us to be reached, too disinterested in what we were doing to care about us.

Some religions say, "Look, this is what you've got to do. You've got to work your way back to God." But how do we do that? How do we work our way back to God? How do we get to be able to stand in His presence? How perfect do we need to be?

The Christian faith tells it this way: God comes down from the castle, as it were, looking for us. He can be found because He is around knocking on the doors of our lives. In anything we experience, however difficult it might be, God may be trying to speak to us. In that moment we may discover that the love of God is real. He is always after us. He is not willing to let us go. He does not want to let us go. He seeks us out.

Ralph Sockman, the Methodist preacher, told of the time he was riding on a horse and fell off. He hit his head, it stunned him, and he lost his sense of direction. He did not know where he was or how to get home. It was getting dark, but he felt one thing, that if he stayed where he was, probably the horse would find its way home. When his father saw the horse, Sockman knew his father would come looking for him. So he sat in the darkness, waiting for his father's voice—until it came.[2]

In the darkness, do we wait for His voice? Sometime in the difficult moments, we will discover that God is surrounding us with love, that God is there waiting for us, ready to help us. We can give thanks in all circumstances because God is seeking to surround us with His great love.

II. We can raise a doxology in difficult times because He may be using these moments to forgive and remake us.

As the disciples came to celebrate the Supper, they remembered how much they had changed. The disciples had to be forgiven a lot to become the disciples they were! Christ was willing to forgive, forget, and then use the experiences to help mold them the way He wanted.

This is the gospel for us. What Christ wants to do is to forgive us of our mistakes and to mold us into something new. In the difficult times as we realize mistakes that have led us to where we are, He is willing to come and forgive us. A young girl went into the pastor's office and told that she was going to have a child. She was afraid to go home again for fear of her father. The pastor went and talked to the father, and the father said in anger, "Never, never can she set foot in my house again." The minister simply said, "Be careful now, because never is a long, long time."[3]

Fortunately, in that circumstance, the father forgave. It's not always that way. Sometimes "never" is said and meant. Sometimes reconciliation does not take place. Sometimes forgiveness does not happen. We may find forgiveness hard, but God is ready to forgive. Whatever we have done against Him, He's ready to forgive it, forget it, and put it in the past. Whatever that sin has been, forgiveness is available. In difficult times we may experience anew the presence of God in forgiveness.

A man working on one of the cathedrals in Europe was carving a piece of wood, a figure, and made a mistake with it. The master craftsman came and saw it and was very angry. Then he took his own tool and began to shape something out of that mess. He began to shape a new figure, a new picture. After he had done it, the master left it to the other man to finish the task. The workman was forgiven for his mistakes, and something new happened because of it.[4]

This is what God does with you and me. Sometimes we are broken, then God takes our brokenness and uses it to shape us and make us something new. Have you become something new because of the forgiveness of God? When you left your sins behind, have you gone on to something better? We can give thanks because of the difficult moments when we leave our sins behind; God uses those moments to reshape us, to renew us.

III. We can give a doxology because in the difficult times we discover a sure and certain hope.

This was what the disciples remembered when they came to celebrate the Supper. They remembered the crucifixion, and it caused despair because the One they loved had been killed; their purpose for living had been shattered. They knew the moment of despair and anguish that we do. When a loved one dies, we don't know how we're going to make it through. We feel so lost in despair. When difficulties of life, frustrations, and disappointment hit us, then we begin to wonder what life is about. Nothing seems to work; it all seems to fall to pieces. As we look at the tragedies that sometimes beset us, we wonder where the meaning is. *What is it about anyway?* We don't know. Life seems confusing and difficult. We can't understand it. We know those moments of despair.

We must never stop at the crucifixion, for this Supper celebrates the resurrection. This was what the disciples came to know. That which seemed to be the worst that could ever happen was turned into something used to bring about the best that could ever happen. The redemption of all humankind. Christ could take the crucifixion and turn it into a resurrection. He could take that which looked bad and bring good out of it.

That's what the gospel is about. In all the difficult experiences of life, God is working to bring something good out of them. When we come to those moments of grief, when we stand at the graveside of those we love, somehow we can hear the voice of Christ crying to us, "Whoever loves Me will not die, but live forever." In the moments of life when we are disappointed and frustrated, and we don't know what it's for, we can hear His voice again saying, "He who loses his life for My sake will find it." To give yourself to love, to give yourself away to peace and justice, and to give yourself away to service is to find what you are here for. When life looks confusing, the voice comes to us, "Don't worry, I'm going to bring it out all right in the end. I'm working to accomplish My purposes. I'm building My kingdom."

Christ tries to take our lives and give them a sure and certain hope, to remind us that nothing can ultimately defeat Him and, therefore, us, if we are His. When we keep our hands in His, He will never let us go.

F. B. Meyer, the English preacher of the last century, traveled miles on the train, preaching everywhere. He never forgot at the end of a trip to go seek out the engineer and thank him for getting him there safely.[5] This is why we can give thanks to God because we know that, as we continue to hold on to Him, one day He will get us safely through this experience of life. He will not let us be derailed if we continue to put our trust in Him. Do we do that? Sometimes in the darkness, you see, we need to remember the Light. That He is at work.

It's hard in all circumstances to give thanks. It's hard to sing, "Praise God from whom all blessings flow," when Christ hangs from a cross. But that's where we can sing it the most because, in that crucifixion, He is expressing His love for us like never before. In that crucifixion, He is sharing with us a forgiveness that we need. In that crucifixion, He gave us the promise of a hope with no cross, no death, no suffering, and no sin too powerful for God. He will take that cross and overcome it with a resurrection.

So we remember today a Body broken and blood shed. We remember a death for us, but we remember most what to be thankful for. God has brought Himself to us through this, has offered Himself to us through this, and whenever we put our lives in His hands, no matter what comes, He will always be with us. Since He is always with us, we can manage to keep on going. We can manage day in and day out to sing, "Praise God from whom all blessings flow." Life is a series of doxologies of praise to God because life has God in it—and with us!

Notes

1. Andrew B. Smither, "Why Was I Born?" *The Pulpit* (July 1958): 21.

2. Glen Edwards, "Preaching from the Book of Acts," *Southwestern Journal of Theology* (Fall 1974): 69.

3. Ernest T. Campbell, "Times When NOT to Pray," *National Radio Pulpit,* n.d., 13.

4. Allan J. Weenink, "The Cunning Craftsman: God," *The New Pulpit Digest* (September-October 1974): 53.

5. W. B. J. Martin, *Little Foxes that Spoil the Vine* (New York: Abingdon Press, 1968), 114.